Top 10 Algarve Highlights

The Top 10 of Everything

TOP 10 ALGARVE

CONTENTS

The Algarve Area by Area

Streetsmart

Within each Top 10 list in this book, no hierarchy of quality or popularity is implied. All 10 are, in the editor's opinion, of roughly equal merit.

Title page, front cover and spine *Rocky outcrops along Ponta da Piedade, Lagos*
Back cover, clockwise from top left *Grilled sardines; sunset at Rio Gilão; a woman traveller in Faro; towering outcrops; sandy beach near Lagos*

The rapid rate at which the world is changing is constantly keeping the DK Eyewitness team on our toes. While we've worked hard to ensure that this edition of the Algarve is accurate and up-to-date, we know that opening hours alter, standards shift, prices fluctuate, places close and new ones pop up in their stead. So, if you notice we've got something wrong or left something out, we want to hear about it. Please get in touch at **travelguides@dk.com**

QUEM
QUER VER
AL416L
INFANTE D HENRIQUE

Welcome to The Algarve

With its golden beaches, fabulous golf courses and year-round appeal, the Algarve is an enticing holiday destination. This enchanting region is famous for its stunning ochre-splashed coastline of shallow bays, vertiginous cliffs and lively resorts, and is also home to a verdant canvas of dramatic hillscapes, quiet villages and sleepy hamlets. With DK Eyewitness Top 10 Algarve, it's yours to explore.

Busiest during the summer, the warm, crystalline waters of the Algarve lure beachgoers to its southern shores. You can hike or cycle nature trails through the serene **Parque Natural da Ria Formosa**, take in spectacular views from the top of **Monchique**, or kayak in the grottoes off **Lagos**. Besides the beautiful landscape, the region has many cultural attractions, including the **Palácio da Galeria** in **Tavira**, the mighty Moorish castle of **Silves** and the gilded medieval interior of **Sé Cathedral** in **Faro**.

Travelling the Algarve's hinterland is to journey through a landscape embroidered with cork-oak and citrus trees, eucalyptus scenting the air. Vineyards are strung across the area and visitors can sample flavours of the region at excellent wineries. On the coast, traditional festivals, fascinating Algarve architecture and markets overflowing with local produce make for a captivating travel experience.

Whether you're visiting for a weekend or a week, our Top 10 guide brings together the best of everything the Algarve has to offer. The guide has useful tips throughout, from seeking out what's free to places off the beaten track, plus six easy-to-follow itineraries, designed to tie together a clutch of sights in a short space of time. An additional chapter on the **Alentejo** highlights the region's neighbouring province. Add inspiring photography and detailed maps, and you've got the essential pocket-sized travel companion. **Enjoy the book, and enjoy the Algarve**.

Clockwise from top: **Praia da Dona Ana, Lagos; Sé Cathedral, Faro; a cobbled street in Alte; boats at Praia dos Pescadores, Albufeira; octopus pots, Santa Luzia; the town of Monchique; Praia dos Pescadores, Albufeira**

Exploring the Algarve

A favourite year-round holiday destination, the Algarve has much to offer visitors. Celebrated for its fantastic beaches and peaceful resorts, the Algarve has an equally enticing interior just waiting to be discovered. Here are a few ideas for a two-day and a week-long stay, which will help you to make the most of coast and country.

Faro Old Town's pretty cobbled streets make for an enjoyable stroll.

Two Days in the Algarve

Day 1

MORNING

Start in **Faro** with some sightseeing in the Old Town *(see pp12–13)*. Ponder ancient artifacts at the Museu Municipal de Faro and follow with a visit to the handsome 13th-century Sé. Afterwards, climb the cathedral's bell tower and enjoy the views across the wetlands.

AFTERNOON

Have lunch at Faz Gostos *(Rua do Castelo 13; 289 878 422)*, and then join a boat cruise *(see pp58–9)* through the protected **Parque Natural da Ria Formosa** *(see pp30–33)*. End the day exploring **Faro's New Town** *(see pp14–15)* and strolling by the riverfront.

Day 2

MORNING

Travel east to **Tavira** *(see pp16–17)* and begin by perusing the Núcleo Islâmico. Climb the hill to the Moorish castle *(see p45)* for splendid rooftop views. Next, look for the tombs of Crusader knights in Igreja de Santa Maria do Castelo. Meander back to the river, the Rio Gilão, and take in views of the photogenic Ponte Romana.

AFTERNOON

Stop for lunch at **Brisa do Rio** *(see p95)* then recharge on **Ilha de Tavira** *(see p94)*, reached by ferry from Quatro Águas quay.

Seven Days in the Algarve

Day 1 and 2

Follow the two-day Algarve itinerary.

Day 3

Travel early to **Loulé** *(see pp22–3)*, timing your visit to coincide with the daily market. Visit the bewitching Ermida de Nossa Senhora da

A vast swathe of golden sand is set against dramatic multicoloured cliffs at Praia da Rocha in Portimão.

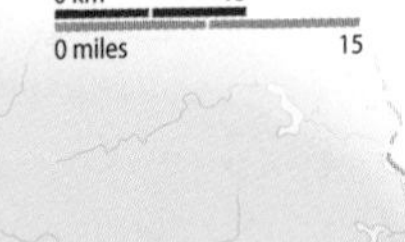

The spa hamlet of Caldas de Monchique has been famous for the restorative powers of its water since Roman times.

Conceição before continuing west to **Albufeira** *(see pp36–7)*. Take some time to relax on Praia da Oura, and then enjoy an evening drink at **Libertos** on the neon-lit "Strip" *(see p81)*.

Day 4

Continue to **Lagos** *(see pp26–7)*, where it is easy to spend a few hours in the fascinating Museu Municipal Dr José Formosinho. Take a cruise to the sea caves at Ponta da Piedade. Back on land, head for the sand on **Meia Praia** *(see p49)*, then enjoy an evening drink at a bar on the **Frente Ribeirinha** *(see p27)*.

Day 5

Drive further west to **Sagres** *(see pp34–5)*. Delve into history at the mysterious Fortaleza de Sagres. Afterwards, follow the bracing Ponta de Sagres Panoramic Walk. Linger in the afternoon on sheltered **Praia do Martinhal** *(see p102)*. For a dramatic finale, drive over to windblown **Cabo de São Vicente** *(see p35)* for awe-inspiring ocean vistas.

Day 6

Journey north through the **Parque Natural do Sudoeste Alentejano e Costa Vicentina** *(see p100)*. Turn inland at **Aljezur** *(see p101)* for the quaint spa hamlet of **Caldas de Monchique** *(see p99)*. Continue to **Monchique** *(see pp20–21)*. Saunter through its steep, narrow streets to shop for *cadeiras de tesoura (see p104)*. End the day with great views from the peak of **Fóia** *(see p20)*.

Day 7

Arrive in **Silves** *(see pp18–19)*. Allow time to absorb the excellent Museu Municipal de Arqueologia. For a more tangible sense of history, amble up to the impressive castle *(see p44)*. Use the afternoon to visit **Portimão** *(see pp38–9)*, before relaxing on Praia da Rocha.

Top 10 Algarve Highlights

The quayside at the village of Ferragudo

TOP 10 Algarve Highlights

The Moors called their al-Gharb the Sunset Land. Blessed with a mild winter climate and lots of sunny days, Portugal's playground province remains one of the most popular year-round holiday destinations in Southern Europe. Lively coastal resorts spill over ribbons of golden sand, whilst quiet, traditional villages can be found inland.

1 Faro

Faro is the capital of the Algarve and an important tourist and commercial centre. Its historic quarter overlooks a marina and the Ria Formosa *(see pp12–15)*.

2 Tavira

Nearly 40 churches can be found in this elegant riverside town, which is one of the prettiest and most romantic places to be found in the Algarve. The Gilão River, spanned by a Roman bridge, flows through the centre *(see pp16–17)*.

3 Silves

Once the grandiose capital of the Moorish province of al-Gharb, Silves today is dominated by the ochre ramparts of its huge castle. Lush orange groves blanket the country-side *(see pp18–19)*.

4 Monchique

The Serra de Monchique rises 458 m (1,500 ft), enveloping the hillside town of Monchique and its neighbouring spa centre *(see pp20–21)*.

5 Loulé

A gateway to the central hinterland and the Caldeirão mountain range, Loulé hosts a daily market and is a thriving centre for the sale of local handicrafts *(see pp22–3)*.

Lagos 6

A young, vibrant and carefree spirit imbues this resort town. The nearby beaches, punctuated with outcrops of sandstone rock, are spectacular *(see pp26–9)*.

7 Parque Natural da Ria Formosa

A sanctuary for a wealth of bird and animal life, this is one of the most important wetland zones in Europe *(see pp30–33)*.

8 Sagres

This town sits on an isolated promontory pounded by the Atlantic. Dramatic views of the ocean from the Cabo de São Vicente *(see pp34–5)*.

Albufeira 9

This is the Algarve's largest resort. Generous beaches flank bustling esplanades brimming with cafés and trendy clubs *(see pp36–7)*.

10 Portimão

Dating back to pre-Roman times, Portimão has an attractive 18th-century town centre and a broad esplanade, which overlooks the River Arade *(see pp38–9)*.

Faro Old Town

Faro's venerable Cidade Velha (Old Town) is the city's most interesting quarter and can be appreciated at a leisurely pace on foot. Set within a circle of medieval walls, the whole vicinity is a veritable time capsule reflecting Faro's brief golden age in the 16th century. The landmark cathedral and cloistered convent are set alongside a patchwork of narrow, cobbled streets with several inviting cafés and shops.

1 Museu Municipal de Faro

Gargoyles in the shape of animals embellish the delightfully secluded Renaissance cloisters of this former convent *(see p46)* **(above)**, now home to the town's archaeological museum. Highlights include a huge Roman floor mosaic and a collection of Moorish oil lamps.

2 Paço Episcopal

The original building was plundered and damaged by the Earl of Essex in 1596. Rebuilt again after the 1755 earthquake, it is still in use today, but closed to the public **(above)**.

3 Igreja de São Francisco

Stunning panels of *azulejos* (painted tiles) depicting the life of St Francis adorn the walls of this church. The vault contains a polychrome panel showing the coronation of the Virgin.

4 Arco da Vila

This grandiose archway to the Old Town was inaugurated in 1812. Tucked inside the arch is an 11th-century horseshoe gate, which is believed to have been built by the Moors and is the only one of its kind in the Algarve.

5 Centro Interpretativo do Arco da Vila

The museum housed within the arch **(right)** chronicles the history of Faro and is set across two floors. The rooftop terrace affords grand views of the monument and the Old Town.

6 Sé (Cathedral)

The interior of the 13th-century cathedral **(below)** reveals a spectacular fusion of the Gothic, Renaissance and Baroque styles: the Capela de Nossa Senhora dos Prazeres, especially, is a jewel of Baroque art, with gilded and lacquered wood carvings, inlaid marble and polished *azulejos*.

7 Igreja da Misericórdia

Built on the site of a 16th-century chapel, the church **(above)** houses a small museum. The highlight is the 17th-century altar, which features a splendid triumphal arch decorated in gilded rococo carvings. Adjoining the church is an 18th-century hospital, but is closed to the public.

9 Galeria Trem

Part of a former military barracks, the Trem art gallery shares floor space with an excavated Roman arch built on Moorish foundations. The venue is a favourite among contemporary artists.

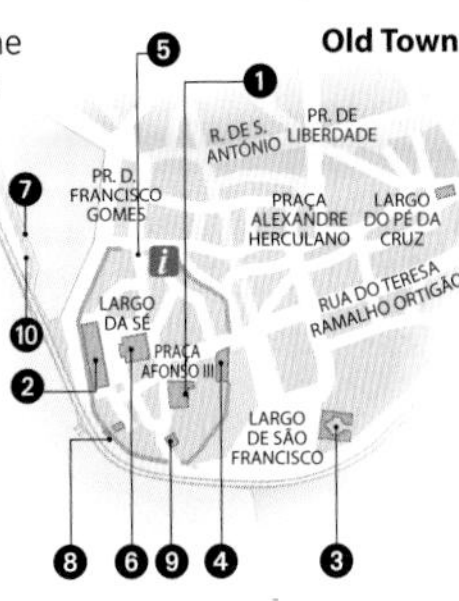

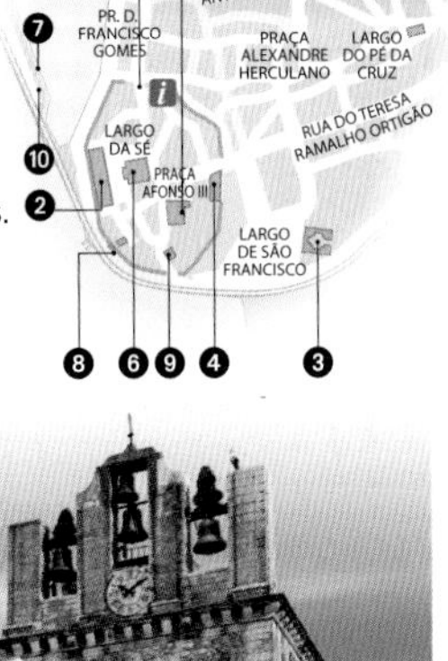

8 Walls and Towers

The original castle walls are vestiges of the Roman occupation of the town, but the rest of the fortifications are the result of 16th-century labour. The exception is the Byzantine towers, added after the collapse of the Roman Empire.

10 Ermida de Nossa Senhora do Ó

The medieval "Chapel of the Pregnant Virgin", is hidden away in the Arco da Vila. It hosts live performances featuring the Portuguese guitar, which is the instrument behind the unique sound of *fado*.

THE STORY OF FARO

The Phoenicians and Carthaginians established trading posts on the banks of the Ria Formosa, which grew into a major Roman port known as Ossonoba. The Moors fortified the town but couldn't halt the armies of Afonso III, who captured the city in 1249. A period of prosperity ended in 1596 when the Earl of Essex burned the city. Rebuilding began, but the 1755 earthquake destroyed it again, forever altering the urban make-up.

NEED TO KNOW

MAP K6

Tourist information: by harbour; (289) 803 604; 10am–6pm daily

Museu Municipal de Faro: Largo Dom Afonso III; 10am–7pm Tue–Fri (6pm winter), 11:30am–6pm Sat & Sun (winter: 10:30am–5pm); adm

Igreja de São Francisco: 10am–noon Mon–Fri

Igreja da Misericórdia: Praça Dom Francisco Gomes 17; 9am–1pm Mon–Fri

Ermida de Nossa Senhora do Ó: noon, 3pm & 4:30pm Sun–Thu; adm (under-12s free)

- **The 16th-century Porta Nova is near the embarkation point for boat cruises on the Ria Formosa** ***(see p59)*****.**
- **The cathedral is free to enter, but you must purchase a ticket to ascend the bell tower.**
- **Entry to the Arco da Vila centre is via the tourist office, with both sharing the same hours.**

Faro New Town and Riverfront

Baroque façade of Igreja do Carmo

1 Igreja do Carmo/ Capela dos Ossos

MAP U1 ■ Largo do Carmo ■ Closed Sun ■ Adm

A feast of Baroque decoration, gilded with the finest Brazilian gold leaf. A macabre offering, though, is the church's Capela dos Ossos (Chapel of Bones), which is lined with the skulls and bones of more than a thousand monks.

2 Teatro Lethes

MAP U2 ■ Rua de Portugal 58 ■ (289) 878 908 ■ www.teatrolethes.com

Once a Jesuit college, this little Italianate gem dates from 1874 and is a beautiful example of a late 19th-century provincial playhouse. It hosts plays and concerts. Guided tours can be arranged.

3 Parque Ribeirinho

MAP K6

Located behind the railway station, Parque Ribeirinho overlooks the Ria Formosa. The park is excellent for walking and cycling.

4 Science Alive Centre

MAP T3 ■ Rua Comandante Francisco Manuel ■ Closed Mon ■ Adm ■ www.ccvalg.pt

An engrossing interactive study centre, which promotes scientific and technological awareness. Climb up to the centre's "observatory" for a voyage into the Milky Way.

5 Faro Jewish Heritage Centre

MAP K5 ■ Estrada da Penha ■ (289) 829 525 ■ Open 9:30am–12:30pm & 2–5pm Mon–Fri

The city's 19th-century Jewish cemetery is laid out in the traditional Sephardic way. The informative Isaac Bitton Synagogue Museum is adjacent to the cemetery, and is decorated with original furniture from 1820.

6 Museu Regional do Algarve

MAP U2 ■ Praça da Liberdade ■ Open 10am–6pm Tue–Fri, 10am–4:30pm Sat ■ Adm

Find out about life in rural Algarve through this display of traditional artifacts. Paintings by Faro artist Carlos Porfírio are also on display here.

Display, Museu Regional do Algarve

7 Ermida de Santo António do Alto

MAP W1 ■ Rua da Berlim

Built in 1355, this is one of the oldest buildings in Faro. A climb up the steps at the side of the chapel rewards visitors with a rooftop view.

8 Ilha de Faro

MAP K6

A natural link in a chain of sand-dune islands that constitute part of the Parque Natural da Ria Formosa *(see pp30–33)*. The estuary side of the beach, with its sheltered waters, is popular with watersports enthusiasts.

9 Palácio Bívar

MAP T2 ■ Rua Conselheiro Bívar

This late 18th-century former private residence, with attractive balconied windows and a grand portal, is generally regarded as the finest example of Neo-Classical architecture in the Algarve.

Mosaics at Villa Romana de Milreu

10 Villa Romana de Milreu

MAP K5

Just 5 km (3 miles) north of Faro, the Roman remains at Milreu *(see p93)* include the ruins of a luxury villa and baths dating from the 2nd century AD.

COSMOPOLITAN FARO

Faro's history *(see p13)* and cosmopolitan flavour continues beyond the obvious Moorish and Christian features of the old town. New townhouses sprang up outside the city walls in the 17th and 18th centuries, Mannerist in style. Battlements built during the War of Restoration (1640–68) enclosed this new urban area. Present day Faro capitalizes on a vibrant social life and a rich artistic heritage. Alluring historical buildings can be found alongside modern museums and quaint pavement cafés. The city boasts a colourful agenda of music and dance; as exciting, in fact, as the city's restaurants, that serve the best traditional cuisine of the Algarve.

Afonso III, King of Portugal

Faro's attractive marina is the starting point for popular boat cruises on the lagoon.

FARO'S TOP 10 PERSONALITIES

1 **Mohammed ben Said ben Hárun** gave Faro its name in the 11th century.

2 **Afonso III** captured the city in 1249.

3 **Samuel Gacon** produced the first printed manuscript in Portugal (1487).

4 **Queen Catarina** completed Convento de Nossa Senhora da Assunção.

5 **The 2nd Earl of Essex** sacked Faro in 1596.

6 **Bishop Francisco Gomes** (1739–1816) rebuilt the city after the quake.

7 **Francisco Xavier Fabri** (1761–1817) was a famous Neo-Classical architect.

8 **Manuel Bívar** (1861–1901) was a key member of an illustrious family.

9 **Dr Amadeu Ferreira de Almeida Carvalho** (1876–1966) gave his art collection to the public.

10 **Carlos Porfírio** (1895–1970) was a renowned modern artist.

Tavira

With its timeless atmosphere, traditional character and dignified charm, it is little wonder that many consider the elegant riverside town of Tavira to be the most pleasant and picturesque in the Algarve. Sited on both sides of the Rio Gilão, the town is perhaps best known for its abundance of churches – nearly 40 in all. Tavira's prosperity today relies to a great degree on tourism, although not to the detriment of the town's peaceful ambience.

1 Castle Remains

The surviving walls of this Moorish fort envelop a spruce garden. The view from the ramparts takes in the town's *(see p45)* pyramid-shaped rooftops and distant Ilha de Tavira.

4 Igreja de Santa Maria do Castelo

The clock face of this church is a familiar landmark **(left)**. Inside are the tombs of the Moors' nemesis, Dom Paio Peres Correia, and seven of his knights.

2 Casa Fotografia Andrade

This permanent exhibition, consisting of photographs taken by the Andrade family, chronicles life in Tavira from the 20th century onwards.

5 Torre de Tavira – Camera Obscura

Housed at the top of an old water tower, the camera obscura focuses a live 360-degree image of the city onto a huge screen.

3 Igreja da Misericórdia

Townsfolk are justifiably proud that this 16th-century church **(below)** is considered to be the Algarve's most important Renaissance monument.

6 Ponte Romana

The foundations of the low, arched stone bridge **(above)** spanning the Rio Gilão are Roman in origin. Illuminated at night, creating a romantic ethereal glow, the bridge is a favourite subject for artists.

7 Ilha de Tavira

A regular ferry service offers an easy escape to the marvellous sand-dune island, which is popular during the summer months for its excellent swimming. It lies within the Parque Natural da Ria Formosa *(see pp30–33)*.

8 Núcleo Islâmico

Tavira's Islamic heritage is featured at this museum. A video presentation outlines the history behind the artifacts, which date from the time when Tavira was ruled by the Moors. The 11th-century Tavira Vase **(right)** is a highlight.

9 Palácio da Galeria

Works by Picasso and Paula Rego have been exhibited at this contemporary gallery, housed in a refurbished 16th-century palace. The palace is set on Moorish foundations, vestiges of which are displayed under a glass floor in the entrance hall.

10 Convento da Graça

Now a luxury *pousada* *(see p123)*, this 16th-century building *(see p126)* **(below)** is characterized by a rich mix of Renaissance and Baroque architecture, with the cloister. The remains of a 12th-century Moorish street can also be seen from the bar.

LOCAL CUISINE

Tavira's seafood specialities include *açorda marisco*, a concoction of cockles, prawns and clams sunk in a thick bread-based soup, and *lulas recheadas*, which is tender squid filled with cured meats and rice, braised in an onion and tomato sauce. Santa Luzia, a village southwest of Tavira, is said to be the Algarve's octopus capital. Order the octopus rice stew *(arroz de polvo)*.

NEED TO KNOW

MAP M4

Tourist information: Praça da República 5; (281) 322 511; open 10am–6pm daily

Casa Fotografia Andrade: Rua da Liberdade 36; (281) 322 102; open 10am–1pm & 3–7pm Mon–Fri, 10am–1pm Sat; adm

Igreja da Misericórdia: open 9am–noon & 2–5pm Mon, 9am–12:30pm & 2–5:30pm Tue–Sun; closed Oct–May: Sun; adm

Torre de Tavira – Camera Obscura: www.torredetavira.com

Núcleo Islâmico: Praça da República; (281) 320 568; open 9:15am–4:30pm Tue–Sat; adm

Palácio da Galeria: Calçada da Galeria; (281) 320 540; open 9:15am–4:30pm Tue–Sat; adm

- **Vila Galé Albacora's Udiving Centre *(see p125)* welcomes divers of all abilities (www.udiving.pt).**
- **Grab drinks and snacks at Café Veneza, on Praça da República.**

Silves

Known as Xelb in Arabic, the 30,000-strong Moorish settlement prospered until 1189, when Dom Sancho I laid siege to it with the help of an English crusader army. The Christians finally gained total control in 1242. These days, Silves is better known as a centre of citrus fruit and cork production. The castle, with its sandstone walls casting a sepia wash over the town below, is a stark reminder of Silves' once-powerful past.

1 Castelo

The grandest monument *(see p44)* to Islamic rule in the Algarve, Silves Castle **(right)** is a huge stronghold built on the site of 4th-century Roman fortifications. Views from the ramparts are superb.

2 Sé (Cathedral)

Dating from the 13th century, the town's Gothic cathedral **(above)** was the seat of the Algarve see until 1577, when that honour was transferred to the bishops' palace in Faro. Curiosities include gargoyles on the apse and Crusader tombs.

3 Museu Municipal de Arqueologia

This fascinating museum *(see p46)* superbly charts human existence in the region from the Palaeolithic period to the 16th century.

4 Ancient Pillory

A common symbol of municipal power across all of Portugal, the pillory standing near the castle was rebuilt from 16th-century remains. Topped by a decorative crown with four sinewy, wrought-iron dragons jutting out from the stem, it is the only example of its kind in the Algarve.

5 Casa da Cultura Islâmica e Mediterrânica

This space **(below)** in Largo de República promotes Silves' rich Islamic legacy and its links to Moorish and Mediterranean culture. It hosts art exhibitions and cultural events. For more details, contact the tourist office.

9 Igreja da Misericórdia

The highly decorative side doorway possibly served as the original entrance to the church **(left)** and shows the influence of the 16th-century Manueline style. The main chapel has a Renaissance altarpiece.

6 Arade River Cruises

The quay near the Roman bridge is where sightseeing boats from Portimão dock *(see p59)*. Look out for herons and flamingoes. Departure times depend on the tide.

7 Ponte Romana

Only the foundations of this very pretty whitewashed bridge date back to Roman times. The rest of the structure is medieval in origin. These days it is closed to traffic.

10 Cruz de Portugal

Standing incongruously next to a main road, this exquisite 16th-century granite cross is said to have been a gift to the city from Dom Manuel I.

8 Quinta do Francês Vineyard

Set in a picturesque valley 6 km (4 miles) northwest of Silves, near Odeluca, this vineyard *(see p72)* offers guided tours and tastings of award-winning reds, whites and rosés.

MOORISH SILVES

As Xelb, Silves was the capital of the Moorish province of al-Gharb and featured several minarets, a set of docks, a shipyard, public baths, a synagogue and a church. By 1053 it had become a crowded metropolis, with writers poets, scientists and philosophers all calling it home. By the mid-12th century, however, Silves started to decline. Nonetheless, the legacy of 500 years of Moorish rule can still be seen in the local architecture and in the fields of orange, almond, fig and carob trees.

NEED TO KNOW

MAP F4

Tourist information: Parque das Merendes; (282) 098 927; open 10am–6pm daily

Museu Municipal de Arqueologia: Rua das Portas de Loulé; 10am–6pm daily (last adm: 5:30pm); adm

Casa de Cultura Islámica e Mediterránica: open only to groups. To arrange a visit, contact tourist information office.

- **A pair of binoculars is useful when scanning the countryside from the castle ramparts.**
- **The Café Inglês, just below the castle, is open daily for home-made fare.**
- **Pastelaria Dona Rosa, just off Rua 25 Abril, fronts a peaceful square, and is decorated with *azulejo* panels.**

Monchique

This pretty little market town nestles in the Serra de Monchique, a densely wooded canvas of eucalyptus, chestnut, pine and cork trees interrupted by tracts of barren moorland. A welcome change from beaches and villas, Monchique is all cobbled streets and rural sentiment. The local *medronho* – firewater distilled from the berries of the Arbutus (strawberry tree) – is the finest available anywhere.

1 Igreja Matriz

An intriguing Manueline doorway **(below)** greets visitors to Monchique's 16th-century parish church. The twisted columns resemble lengths of gnarled rope. Inside, the capitals of the columns in the three naves are similarly fashioned, suggesting a nautical theme.

2 Galeria de Santo António

This engaging art gallery, housed in a former 18th-century hermitage, hosts live music events as well as exhibitions featuring works by local and international artists.

3 Villa Termal das Caldas de Monchique Spa Resort

Set under a canopy of pine and eucalyptus, this modern thermal spa complex **(right)** retains a nostalgic air *(see p127)*.

The attractive market town of Monchique

4 Fóia

For the most spectacular landscape views in the Algarve, head for the peak of Fóia. At 902 m (2,959 ft), this is the highest point in the Serra da Monchique. You can either drive or walk up along a well-marked path.

5 Barranco dos Pisões

An idyllic little beauty and picnic spot in the woods about 4 km (2 miles) northwest of Monchique, the Barranco dos Pisões is known locally for its ancient water wheel and its 150-year-old plane tree.

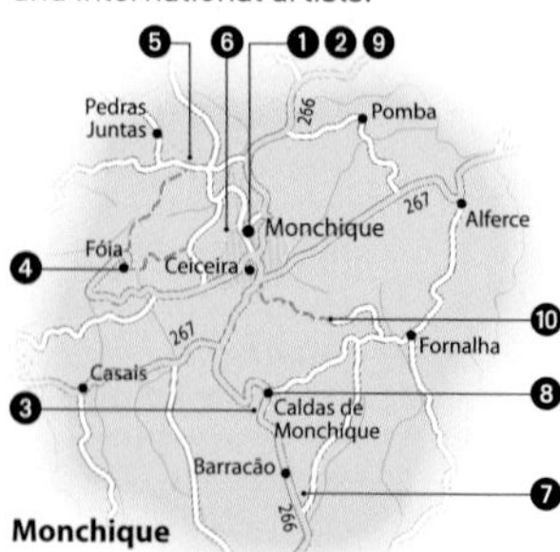

6 Nossa Senhora do Desterro

A mysterious air pervades the ruins of the Franciscan monastery **(above)**. Severely damaged by the 1755 earthquake, its empty shell echoes with the rustle of leaves from an immense magnolia tree standing in the old garden. The interior is closed to the public.

7 Parque da Mina

Centred around a disused iron-ore mine, this imaginative theme park *(see p64)* features a lovingly restored 18th-century manor house and a traditional distillery. There is also a playground and a nature trail, with picnic areas along the way.

8 Caldas de Monchique

The Romans were bowled over by this little hamlet in the Monchique hills, and totally impressed by the hot, curative properties of its waters **(above)**.

MONCHIQUE'S SPA

According to legend, if you take a sip from the fountain of love, an ancient font hiding in the dappled woods behind Caldas de Monchique, you'll fall in love with life. The waters are said to be good for a whole host of maladies, including rheumatic and digestive disorders and skin complaints. The Romans certainly thought so, as did Dom João II. Today's visitors are offered a range of water-based therapies, using vapours, water jets, hydromassage, steam and hot algae.

9 Igreja de São Sebastião

The church **(below)** contains a beautifully sculpted 17th-century figure of Nossa Senhora do Desterro.

10 Picota

At 773 m (2,536 ft), the Algarve's second-highest peak doesn't quite command the same all-round vista as Fóia, but Picota is steeper and pleasantly wooded. Its location offers beautiful views that take in long sweeps of scented meadows and a sparkling, distant sea to the south.

NEED TO KNOW

MAP E3 ■ Visitor information: Largo S. Sebastião; (282) 911 189

Open 10am–6pm Mon–Fri

Galeria de Santo António: Calçada de St. António; open only during special exhibitions and events

■ **For a pleasant walk, follow the terraced footpath in the grounds of the spa complex.**

■ **Monchique is also known for its small wooden "scissor" chairs, which make good gifts.**

■ **Reasonably priced cafés and restaurants cluster round the central bus station.**

■ **Down in Caldas de Monchique, Café-Restaurante 1692 has a marvellous terrace that spills out onto the square, making it a good choice.**

TOP 10 Loulé

The pleasant inland town of Loulé is renowned for its traditional handicrafts and splendid market. The Romans first settled on the spot now occupied by the castle, but it was the Moors for whom Loulé was to become a place of some importance. Remnants of their presence can still be seen in the bell tower of Igreja Matriz de São Clemente, formerly a minaret. The castle is also Moorish in origin. Almonds and figs have been essential to the local economy for centuries.

1 Museu Municipal de Loulé

The highlight of this museum **(above)** is the first-floor recreation of a traditional Algarve kitchen, complete with 19th-century utensils and tableware *(see p47)*.

2 Igreja Matriz de São Lourenço

About 8 km (5 miles) southeast of Loulé, at Almancil, blue and white *azulejo* panels adorn the walls of the chancel, nave and the magnificent trompe-l'oeil cupola of this decorative church.

3 Castelo

The ruins of this fortress underwent restoration during the 19th century, and today the castle **(right)** houses a museum *(see p45)*. Visitors are rewarded with grand views of the town from its battlements.

4 Pólo Museológico dos Frutos Secos

This original museum focuses on early harvesting methods for figs, carob and almond fruit. It was built in homage to a local businessman.

5 Ermida de Nossa Senhora da Conceição

This 16th-century chapel **(left)** is decorated with *azulejos* and has a stunning Baroque altarpiece. The ceiling panel is by the Loulé painter Rasquinho.

NEED TO KNOW

MAP J4 ■ Visitor Information: Ave 25 de Abril 9; (289) 463 900

Pólo Museológico dos Frutos Secos: Rua Gil Vincente 14

Loulé Carnival: in Feb (Shrove Tuesday)

Market: Praça da República; open 7am–3pm daily

Igreja Matriz de São Lourenço: **MAP J5**; Rua do Igreja, Almancil

■ When the Islamic bathhouse is closed, ask for the key at Rua Vice Almirante Cândido dos Reis 36; (289) 400 642.

■ Rua de 5 Outubro has many bars, cafés and shops.

■ Order a *bica* (small coffee) at the historic Café Calcinha *(Praça da República 67)*.

6 Galeria de Arte do Convento do Espírito Santo

The decorated and vaulted ceilings of this former convent provide a splendid setting for the selection of contemporary paintings, sculptures and conceptual installations that are on display inside. There are regular contributions from local and international artists.

8 Igreja Matriz de São Clemente

Loulé's Muslim faithful were once summoned to prayer from the balcony of the lofty bell tower, which originally served as a minaret. Other highlights are the Capela de Nossa Senhora da Consolação and the Capela de São Brás's Baroque altarpiece.

TRADITIONAL CRAFTS

It was the inauguration of an artisans' fair back in 1291 that forged Loulé's reputation as a manufacturing centre. Many of the techniques used 800 years ago are still employed today. Ceramics are popular with tourists. In many local villages, residents still plait the leaves of dwarf palms to make hats, baskets and rugs; jute fibre is used to stitch pretty rag dolls. Saddleries tucked away in quiet hamlets supply harnesses for mules, and old wooden looms are used to produce shawls and blankets.

9 Banhos Islâmicos

The well-preserved ruins of an Islamic bathhouse known as *hammam de Al-'Ulyà* can be admired from a public viewing platform above the foundations, which date from the 1200s.

7 Loulé Carnival

The biggest, brightest and rowdiest of the Algarve's carnivals. Costume-clad revellers shake, rattle and roll for three days and nights to hybrid Latin rhythm and African-style percussion.

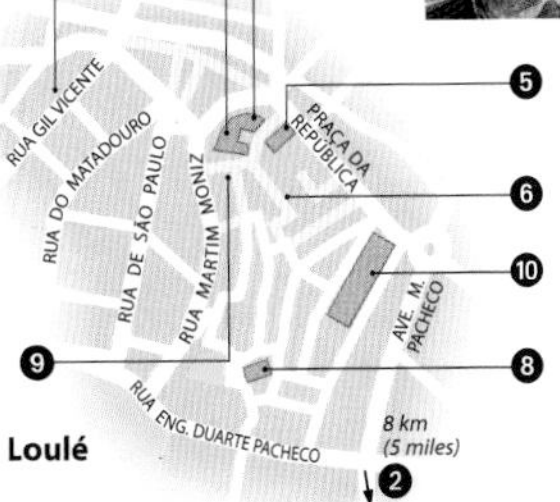

10 Market

Mixed herbs, cheeses and red chilli peppers are sold alongside sweet figs, marzipan cakes and golden honey. Elsewhere, flowers, the freshest of fish, the ripest of fruit and a variety of genuine handicrafts **(above)**, make a visit to Loulé market an unforgettable shopping experience.

Following pages *Panoramic view of Silves*

Lagos

Vibrant and busy with holidaymakers, Lagos is probably the most popular destination in the Algarve. Lagos's name literally means "lakes" in Portuguese – a fitting name for the town's coastal location. This coastal town, an important naval centre in the 15th century, was also where the slave trade first found its roots in Europe. Today, it is known for its lovely beaches, sandstone cliffs, bargain-stacked shops, bars, restaurants and the relaxed atmosphere.

1 Igreja de Santo António

This 18th-century church is a jewel in the Algarve crown. Its gilded and painted woodwork overflows with opulence. Everything the Baroque age is famous for is here: double-chinned cherubs, mythical beasts and ripened fruit. Entry is via the Museu Municipal Dr José Formosinho.

3 Forte da Ponta da Bandeira

Accessible via a drawbridge, this 17th-century fortress **(above)** was built to defend the harbour. Its ramparts now protect a small museum dedicated to the Age of Discoveries.

2 Igreja de Santa Maria

The town's parish church **(above)** dates back to the 16th century, although much of what you see today was rebuilt in the 19th century. The church, however, still retains its Renaissance doorway with Doric columns and busts of São Pedro (St Peter) and São Paulo (St Paul) on either side of the archivolt.

4 Ponta da Piedade

Parts of the dramatic headland **(below)**, 3 km (2 miles) northwest of the town, resemble a huge wedge of crumbling ginger cake. Beneath gnarled sandstone cliffs, towering outcrops of umber-hued rock rise up, hiding a warren of caves and grottoes. The lighthouse is a prime spot from which to watch the sunset.

5 Museu Municipal Dr José Formosinho

This museum houses an extraordinary collection of artifacts and oddities, plus one or two national treasures *(see pp28–9)*. Of note are the Roman mosaics and a collection of intricately carved and hand-painted model fishing boats.

6

7 Marina de Lagos

With 462 pontoon berths for yachts up to 30 m (100 ft) long, this first-class marina **(left)** enjoys an international reputation. Distinguished with several awards, including a European Blue Flag, it is also known for its bars, restaurants and cafés. Several coastal- and river-cruise companies are based here.

10 Praia do Camilo

A long wooden staircase leads down to this delightful wedge of golden sand, hemmed in by a series of ornate rock formations in rich ochre tones. Craggy stacks, the colour of gingerbread, rise out of the shallows and create a natural shelter against the wind. Countless seabirds find shelter here.

Slave Market Site 8

The northeastern corner of Praça Infante Dom Henrique **(right)** was the site of Europe's first slave market in the 15th century.

6 Town Walls

The foundations of the town walls date from Roman times, and were strengthened during Arab and Christian occupation. Restored in the 16th century, the best-preserved section encases a Manueline window from which Dom Sebastião *(see p29)* is said to have addressed townsfolk before going to Alcácer Quibir.

9 Monte da Casteleja Organic Farm and Vineyard

This charming estate promotes organic farming and produces fine wine. Just 4 km (2 miles) east of the city centre, the winery *(see p73)* sits in stunning rolling countryside, where a traditional farmhouse serves as a wine-tasting centre.

NEED TO KNOW

MAP D5 ■ Tourist office: Praça Gil Eanes; (282) 763 031

Museu Municipal Dr José Formosinho: Rua General Alberto Silveira; open 9:30am–12:30pm & 2–5pm Tue–Sun; adm

Slave Market Museum: Praça do Infante Dom Henrique; open: 10am–12:30pm & 2–5:30 pm Tue–Sun; adm

■ For a boat trip to the grottoes, embark from Avenida dos Descobrimentos, in front of the marina. On this route you will pass Dona Ana beach.

■ At the site of the slave market and in the middle of the square, there is a small museum that examines the role of Lagos in the slave trade.

Highlights of Lagos Museu Municipal Dr José Formosinho

Visitors at Museu Municipal Dr José Formosinho

Opus Vermiculatum Mosaic

This impressive, near-complete Roman mosaic was unearthed in 1933 by the museum's founder, Dr José Formosinho, near Budens, around 10 km (6 miles) west of Lagos. Complementing it is a smaller example discovered at Abicada, 2 km (1 mile) east of Portimão.

Senhora do Forte Model Village

Housed in the Ethnographic Hall is a remarkable labour of love: a huge scale model of an imaginary Algarve coastal town. Constructed with breathtaking attention to detail, it took Lagos resident Pedro Reis 5,300 hours to build over a three-year, seven-month period.

Model of an imaginary Algarve village

Traditional Portuguese Boats

This impressive collection of 28 miniature boats was skilfully carved out of wood and hand-painted by local artisan, Arez Viegas. The models include barges, launches, fishing boats and steamers. The prize exhibit is the frigate, *D. Fernando II e Glória*.

Altar de Campanha

An extraordinary 17th-century mobile altar that was carried by Portuguese troops into the field and used for prayer between military engagements. A carved statue of St Anthony rests on top of the altar, which is inlaid with gold leaf.

São Gonçalo de Lagos

A delightful anomaly, the 18th-century statue of Lagos' patron saint is incorporated into the door of a cupboard that was used by the priests of the time to store their robes.

6 Priests' Vestments

A number of fine examples of priests' vestments are displayed in the Sacred Art wing of the museum, but the most outstanding garment is the one worn at a Mass attended by King Dom Sebastião I soon before his death. The crusading king perished on the Moroccan battlefield along with 8,000 of his troops in 1578. The robe is hand-embroidered with gold.

7 Foral Dado a Lagos (Town Charter)

Presented to Lagos by Dom Manuel I in 1504, the facsimile on display is of the opening page of the rare manuscript, embossed with gold leaf.

DOM MANVEL
Per graça de deos Rey de portugall
dos allgarues daquē ⁊ dalem maar e
africa Senhor deguinee ⁊ da Cōquista
navegaçam ⁊ comercio de etiopia arab
persia ⁊ da india ⁊c. A quantos e
ta nossa carta deforall dada anossa
dita villa de lagos virem fazemos sa
ber que vendo Nos como ho officio

The beautifully illustrated Foral Dado

8 Portrait of Estevão Amarante

The life-sized portrait (not always on display) of the late Portuguese thespian, Estevão Amarante, is by Fernando Santos. As you walk past the image, the change in perspective appears to make Sr Amarante's left foot move with you – a very eerie sensation.

9 Cork Altarpiece

A masterpiece of cork whittling, this framed, three-dimensional retable was carved by Silves resident, Francisco Figueiras in 1907. Its filigree decoration is extremely delicate.

STORY OF LAGOS

Lagos has welcomed visitors ever since the Phoenicians and Carthaginians established settlements along the banks of its natural harbour more than 2,000 years ago. Under subsequent Roman occupation, the town became known as Lacobriga, and flourished as a busy trading port. The Moors built a double ring of ramparts around its centre during their occupation of the area, but that was not enough to repel the Christians who conquered the city in 1241.

During the 15th century – the period of Portugal's Golden Age of Discoveries – Henry the Navigator's caravels departed Lagos shipyards bound for far-flung African regions, and the town quickly became a centre for trade in ivory, gold, silver and other exotic merchandise. Unfortunately, a far more unsavoury enterprise was also spawned: the transatlantic slave trade.

Lagos became the capital of the Algarve in 1576 and remained so until 1756, when the honour was transferred first to Tavira, and then finally to Faro. By that time, however, much of the Algarve, Lagos included, lay in ruins after the devastating 1755 earthquake, a fact that seems unimaginable today.

10 Igreja de Santo António

After visiting the museum, it is worth taking time to appreciate the adjacent church. The opulent 18th-century interior, with its spectacular excess of gilded Baroque carvings, *azulejo* panels and decorated ceiling, is extravagant and impressive, and its finery is a compelling sight.

TOP 10 Parque Natural da Ria Formosa

The Parque Natural da Ria Formosa comprises an extensive lagoon that follows 60 km (37 miles) of coastline between Manta Rota and Vale do Lobo. Made up of sand-dune islands, marshland, saltpans and freshwater lakes, the habitat provides sanctuary for an astonishing assortment of flora and fauna, including birds such as white storks and the rare purple gallinule. The park's headquarters are located at Quinta de Marim, 3 km (2 miles) east of Olhão.

1 Quinta do Lago Nature Trail

This partly shaded trail highlights the flora of two widely differing ecosystems: woodland and salt marshland. The path winds past umbrella and maritime pines.

Aerial view of Parque Natural da Ria Formosa

2 São Lourenço Nature Trail

One of the most rewarding introductions to the reserve is to follow the 3-km (2-mile) São Lourenço nature trail **(above)**. It will bring you into close contact with two different types of wetland: the salt marshes and the freshwater lagoons.

3 Roman Salting Tanks

Five Roman salting tanks **(right)** can be explored near the freshwater lagoons. Dating from the 2nd century AD, they were once used for salting fish prior to their distribution all over Rome's empire

4 Recuperation Centre for Animals

This hospital and rehabilitation centre for sick and injured animals has an area where visitors can obtain more information about the Algarve's wildlife and the animals being treated here.

5 Tide Mill

Tide mills were once very common in the lagoon and estuaries along the Portuguese coastline. Power was obtained by utilizing the change in water levels associated with shifting tides. The example on the Ria Formosa **(right)** is the last of 30 that used to operate.

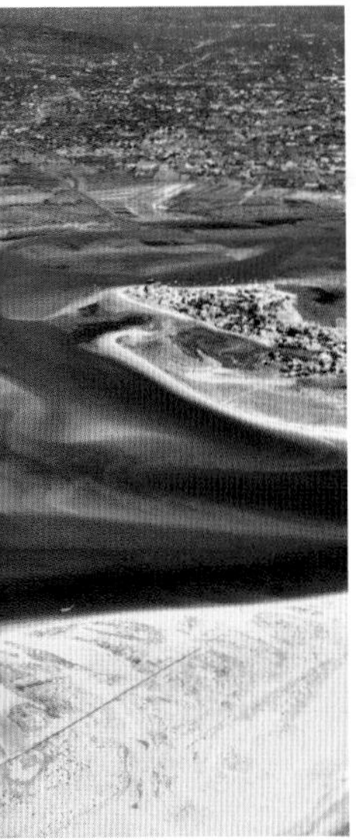

6 Coastal Dunes

The sweeping tracts of sand **(below)** guarding the mouth of the estuary constitute a fragile environment, partly held together by the vegetation that has colonized them.

7 Freshwater Lagoons and Hides

The freshwater lagoons provide vital refuge for nesting and migrating birds, and harbour a miscellany of aquatic mammals. The views from the observation hides bring this sparkling marine oasis into sharp focus.

8 Olhão Nature Trail

The longest trail in the reserve meanders past a tide mill, the remains of Roman salting tanks and several wildlife observation hides before looping back to the park's headquarters.

9 Ecoteca Museu João Lúcio

João Lúcio, 19th-century poet, lawyer and former mayor of Olhão, owned much of the land on which Quinta de Marim is now situated. His former villa, near the river's edge, is now an ecomuseum.

10 Coastal Conifer Woods

Coastal conifer woodland is sparse in the eastern Algarve, but where it occurs it provides an efficient means of coastal protection and adds to the diverse beauty of the terrain.

NEED TO KNOW

MAP K–L6 ■ Park headquarters: Quinta de Marim; call (289) 700 210 for information about volunteering and conservation projects

Park: open 9am–8pm Mon–Fri, 10am–6:30pm Sat & Sun (winter: to 5:30pm)

Ecoteca Museu João Lúcio: (289) 700 940; open 9am–12:30pm & 2–5:30pm Mon–Fri

- **It is advisable to wear a pair of sturdy walking boots if you are planning to follow the nature trails. You will need to put on warm clothing in winter.**
- **Photographers in the hides will need a telephoto lens of at least 300 mm.**
- **The Vista Formosa restaurant opposite the park's main entrance serves a good selection of fresh grilled fish.**

Wildlife of the Ria Formosa

Purple gallinule by the lagoon

1 Purple Gallinule

Very rare, this striking bird is reclusive in nature and tends to play hide-and-seek in the cattail that sprouts along the edge of the freshwater lagoons. A dark-coloured relative of the moorhen, there are numerous couples in residence.

2 Kentish Plover

Found at large along the eastern Algarve coastline, this small wading bird is a talented actor. If you stray too close to its nesting site, it will drag one wing along the ground as if it has been injured, to lure intruders away from its young.

Hoopoe

3 Mediterranean Chameleon

This is a treat indeed for anyone lucky enough to spy one of these remarkable creatures, with its colour-coordinated skin. Hibernating from December to March, the best time to see this bulbous-eyed reptile out and about is on early spring mornings.

4 European Pond Terrapin

A whimsical little member of the chelonian family, this diminutive amphibian is fond of lakes, ponds and calm rivers. It is usually only detected as it darts for shelter at the sound of approaching feet. Tread lightly when you are on the look-out for these creatures.

5 Azure-Winged Magpie

A handsome, cheeky bird frequently heard chattering in small groups among the pinewoods near Quinta do Lago. Easily recognizable by its sooty crown and nape, the blue flash of its wing feathers makes this species particularly alluring in flight.

6 Viperine Snake

The great pretender, this snake is distinguished by its zigzag dorsal line and chestnut-coloured scales, which imitate those of a viper. If disturbed it will rear up, inflate its neck and spit. However, it is all theatrics – the snake is completely harmless.

7 Hoopoe

An exotic-looking bird with a lovely salmon-pink crest, the hoopoe is the golfer's companion, often seen probing for cutworm on the manicured grass of fairways across the Algarve. Primarily a summer visitor, some individuals remain in the region throughout the winter.

8 Greater Flamingo

There is not a sight more majestic than a band of flamingoes panning for food on the salinas. Large flocks of these graceful birds gather in the park

Greater flamingo

during autumn, en route to winter breeding grounds, but they can also be spotted in the summer.

9 Little Tern

The little tern's favoured nesting site in Portugal is along the Ria Formosa, but the fact that it nests on the sand means that breeding is, at best, precarious.

10 Fiddler Crab

Often seen scuttling in panic across the mud at low tide, the male of the species has one of its pincers (left or right) considerably more developed than the other. Its European distribution is confined wholly to the Iberian peninsula.

The distinctive fiddler crab

PRESERVING THE ENVIRONMENT

For those visitors who want to spend more time at the wonderful Ria Formosa and help to preserve and conserve its varied wildlife, the Centro de Educação Ambiental de Marim (Marim Environmental Educational Centre – CEAM) works to protect the environment and promote a balanced, sustainable development of the park's natural resources. It runs a number of projects manned by volunteers, and members of the public are welcome to join in its efforts. Assisting at the Wildlife Recovery Centre, where sick and injured wild birds and animals are nurtured back to health, is one of the most popular programmes. There is a waiting list to join the team of volunteers, and those interested in this, or any of CEAM's other projects, should call (289) 700 210 or check www.natural.pt.

The salt marshes and lagoons of the Parque Natural da Ria Formosa are a haven for a wide variety of flora and fauna.

TOP 10 PLANTS IN THE PARK

Dunes

1 Marram grass (helps to support the dune)

2 Sea holly (top of dune)

3 Thrift (centre of dune)

4 Sea daffodil (delicate white flowers in summer)

Coastal Woodland

5 Furze (thorny shrub)

Salt Marsh

6 Cord grass (endures long submersion)

7 Sea lavender (identified by spikes of white, pink or mauve flowers)

8 Sea purslane (lance-shaped leaves and purple flowers)

Freshwater Lagoon

9 Cattail (cylindrical spike)

10 Rush (ideal shelter for aquatic wildlife)

TOP 10 Sagres

In summer, this small harbour town overflows with youngsters armed with surfboards and a *joie de vivre*. Crammed with welcoming *pensões*, it is an excellent base from which to explore the fine beaches spread along the Algarve's untamed west coast. Sagres is the most southwesterly community in continental Europe, and its laid-back atmosphere is infectious.

1 Fortaleza de Santo António de Beliche

Perched on a pinnacle overlooking the Atlantic Ocean, this 17th-century fortification **(below)** also contains a small chapel, which in turn marks the site of an even earlier ruined church.

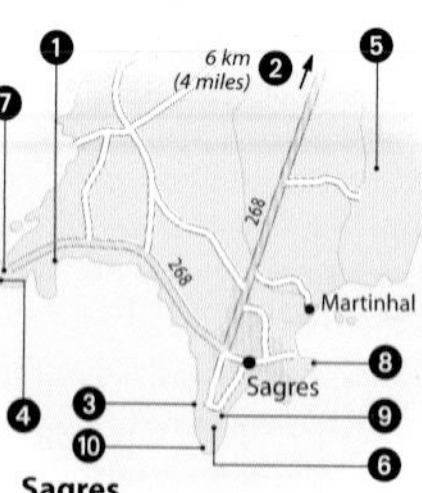

2 Menhir Circuit

Starting near Hortas do Tabual, this 2 km (1 mile) circular walk passes a series of *menhirs*, or megaliths – monumental stones that date back to 3000 BC.

3 Nossa Senhora da Graça

The foundations of this graceful 16th-century chapel, facing Cabo de São Vicente, are said to have been laid by Prince Henry the Navigator.

NEED TO KNOW

MAP B6 ■ Visitor information: located about 1 km (half a mile) from the fishing harbour at Rua Comandante Matoso; (282) 624 873

Open Mon–Fri

Fortaleza de Sagres: open Nov–Mar: 9am–5:30pm; May, Jun & Sep: 9:30am–8pm (Apr–Oct: to 6:30pm; Jul & Aug: to 8:30pm); adm

■ **Enjoy views from the Ponta da Atalaia and the Praia da Mareta.**

■ **Try Dromedário (Rua Comandante Matoso), or Pastelaria Marreiros (Praça da República) for a mid-morning bite.**

■ **The restaurant at Pousada de Sagres is perfect to enjoy regional seafood specialities.**

4 Cabo de São Vicente

The forbidding look of this windblown cape **(right)** is quite awe-inspiring *(see p100)*. Greek historian Strabo, writing at the time of Christ, believed it to be the end "of all the inhabited earth".

5 Parque Natural do Sudoeste Alentejano e Costa Vicentina

This wild and beautiful park **(above)** covers nearly all of the western coast of the Algarve *(see p100)*. It protects a complex ecosystem and lies under a busy migratory flight path for birds.

6 Fortaleza de Sagres

Ominous, stark and, in its time, virtually impregnable, two solid bastions and massive front walls are the impressive hallmarks of this 18th-century fort *(see p45)*. Little else resembles a defensive structure today, except perhaps the mighty cliffs themselves.

7 Farol do Cabo de São Vicente

The tidy buildings around this lighthouse *(farol)* incorporate a small museum, snack bar and gift shop. The tower is closed to the public but the fortifications offer majestic views of the coastline.

8 Forte da Baleeira

A crumbling wall and arch are virtually all that remain of the harbour fortification, but the coastal view from the headland is superb.

HENRY THE NAVIGATOR (1394–1460)

A scholarly and devout man, Prince Henry is said to have brought together the most learned of astronomers and astrologers, skilled cartographers and geographers, and the very best boat designers, to create a school of navigation known as Vila do Infante. Although he didn't sail himself, he laid the foundation of Portugal's maritime expansion. He oversaw and sponsored many expeditions, mapping the way for Portugal's Golden Age of Discoveries.

10 Ponta de Sagres Panoramic Walk

A bracing walk can be enjoyed around the edge of the promontory. Next to the lighthouse is a vast blowhole where you can hear the pounding of the ocean as it crashes into the rocks far below.

9 Rosa dos Ventos

The extraordinary giant wind rose, or wind compass – a device used for measuring the direction of the wind – is said to have been built for Prince Henry the Navigator, although it may actually date from the 16th century. It is an impressive 43 m (141 ft) in diameter. The intriguing circle and its radiating points have been marked by pebbles **(above)**.

Albufeira

Albufeira is one of Portugal's most popular holiday destinations and the largest resort town in the Algarve. Famed for its fabulous beaches and nightlife, the town gets very busy in summer, when it positively bursts with energy. Its history is just as animated, from Roman settlement 2,000 years ago, Arab and Christian conquest in the 8th and 13th centuries respectively, to its rise and fall as a centre of trade and the emergence of its fishing industry.

1 Praia dos Pescadores

"Beach of the Fishermen" **(above)** is so named because of the many fishing vessels left on the sand between use. The grizzled fishermen who own the boats seem oblivious to the sunbathers who descend on this well-known beach in summer.

2 Castle Walls

The mighty ramparts that once surrounded Albufeira crumbled to dust as the 1755 earthquake struck. A corner wall, the North Door, does survive though, in Rua Joaquim Pedro Samora. A remnant of St Anne's Gate also still stands, which forms part of a restaurant interior today.

3 Igreja de São Sebastião

The altarpiece is the shining star of this exquisite church. Its gilded form presides over a 14th-century statue of Nossa Senhora da Orada, who is shown clutching a baby Jesus.

4 Museu Municipal de Arqueologia

Peer closely and you'll spy some charming exhibits **(below)** at this museum. Highlights include Roman earrings and a 7th-century Visigoth earthenware wine goblet *(see p47)*.

5 Galeria Pintor Samora Barros

Named in honour of the artist/poet whose diligent handiwork adorns the parish church in Albufeira, this airy gallery overlooking the town square stages work by contemporary Portuguese and international artists.

Albufeira
7 6 km (4 miles)
5
RUA DA LIBERDADE
RUA 5 DE OUTUBRO
LARGO ENG. D. PACHECO
R. PADRE S. AZEVEDO
RUA ALVES CORREIA
AVENIDA 25 DE ABRIL
R CÂNDIDO DOS REIS
2 km (1 mile) 9 10
8 3 km (2 miles)
RUA M. BOMBARDA
R. J. P. SAMORA
R. H. CALADO
3
R. LATINO COELHO
Tunnel
TR. DA BATERIA
PRAÇA DO PESCADOR
Praia do Peneco
6 2 km (1 mile)
4 2 1

⑥ Marina de Albufeira

The marina **(below)**, located 4 km (2 miles) west of the resort, is the departure point for sightseeing cruises, diving expeditions and fishing excursions. It is also home to a number of good bars and restaurants.

⑦ Adega do Cantor

Owned by British singer Sir Cliff Richard, this vineyard **(left)** lies 6 km (4 miles) northwest of Albufeira, behind the Algarve Shopping mall *(see p74)*. Pre-booked guided tours include tastings *(see p72)*, which are held in the well-stocked shop.

⑧ Parque Aventura

The Adventure Park features high-rope obstacle courses for a range of age groups (starting at the age of four), set at varied heights within the trees. There is also a paintball area.

WATERSPORTS

The crystal-clear waters of the Atlantic provide the Algarve with a thriving watersports scene. Fun begins with the humble pedalo, but for the more sea-hardy a diving centre (www.easydivers.pt) at Marina de Albufeira is great for beginners. For kids, the Leãozinho pirate ship (www.dreamwavealgarve.com) explores the nearby grottoes. Praia da Galé, about 6 km (4 miles) west, is known for its jet- and water-skiing, while windsurfers and paragliders head for Praia da Falésia.

⑨ Praia da Oura

Albufeira's "Golden Beach" fringes the village-resort of the same name, giving it the advantage of proximity to shops and cafés.

⑩ "The Strip"

Glitzy, gaudy and totally irresistible, this is Albufeira's mini Las Vegas: a narrow, neon-lit runway of hotels and restaurants, pubs, cafés and bars, with the odd *artesanato* (craft shop) squeezed in. Two of the region's top nightclubs, Kiss and Libertos, are found here.

NEED TO KNOW

MAP G5 ■ Tourist information office: Rua 5 de Outubro 8; (289) 585 279

Parque Aventura: (913) 185 782; open mid-Jun–mid-Sep: 10am–6pm daily; mid-Sep–mid-Jun: 2–6pm daily.

■ Albufeira bus station is 2 km (1 mile) north of the old town. Almost all buses from the resort arrive or depart from here. Visit www.algarvebus.info for more details on facilities and timetables *(see p117)*.

■ Albufeira is awash with bars and cafés, but those lining Largo Cais Herculano are particularly appealing. Try Cabana Fresca, right in front of Praia dos Pescadores, known for its tasty seafood snacks.

Portimão

Once the centre of the region's fishing industry, Portimão is better known today as a vibrant tourism hub. The old town's 18th-century veneer, the landscaped riverfront and several highly regarded visitor attractions help to showcase this busy port. Leisure options, meanwhile, include a fabulous beach, an international marina and a fascinating offshore diving site.

1 Marina de Portimão

At the mouth of the Rio Arade, the marina **(above)** provides 620 pontoon berths for watercraft up to 50 m (165 ft). Shops, restaurants and bars line the boardwalk near the beach.

2 Museu de Portimão

Occupying a former cannery, this award-winning museum **(above)** traces the town's prehistoric, Roman and Islamic heritage *(see p47)*. Its fish-canning industry is also explored.

3 Teatro Municipal de Portimão

This first-class performing arts venue stages regular music concerts, theatre productions and contemporary dance acts. There is also a café upstairs.

4 Monumentos Megalíticos de Alcalar

One of the region's most important archaeological sites lies 10 km (6 miles) away at Alcalar. A 5,000-year-old megalithic burial chamber is the main sight.

6 Quinta da Penina

Guided tours of the winery *(see p87)* followed by tastings can be booked in advance at this highly regarded vineyard, situated 8.5 km (5 miles) northwest of Portimão. Prices vary depending on the number of participants.

5 Autódromo Internacional do Algarve

Prestigious motorsport tournaments and a classic-car festival *(see p76)* are hosted at this racetrack **(below)**, 15 km (9 miles) north of Portimão.

7 Praia da Rocha

Praia da Rocha **(below)** is named after its beach *(see p49)*, one of the most impressive in the Algarve. The resort's plethora of hotels, nightclubs and restaurants is a magnet for Portimão residents and holiday-makers.

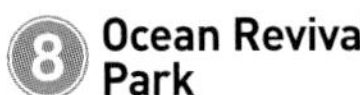

8 Ocean Revival Park

Submerged 4 km (2 miles) off the coast are four decommissioned navy vessels sunk to create a fascinating artificial reef. You can explore the site through diving centres certified by the park *(see p82)*.

MARITIME HERITAGE

Portimão's history is bound up with the river and the sea. The Romans settled here for the Arade Waterway, a valuable gateway between the Mediterranean and the Atlantic. In the modern era, a prosperous fishing and canning industry developed. Inevitably, the passage of time saw fish stocks depleted and factories closed down. The tide turned, however, with the rise in tourism. Today, a fleet of sightseeing boats navigate the estuary, and the town welcomes cruise liners from around the world.

9 Igreja de Nossa Senhora da Conceição

Little is left of the original church **(left)**, destroyed in the 1755 earthquake *(see p43)*. The portico, however, survived and remains a fine example of 15th-century architecture.

10 Igreja do Antigo Colégio da Companhia de Jesus

The imposing pyramid-like façade of this remarkable 17th-century structure provides the old town with a unique architectural reference point. The interior features Baroque altarpieces and the tomb of Diogo Gonçalves, the church's founder.

NEED TO KNOW

MAP E4 ■ Visitor information: Teatro Municipal de Portimão, Largo 1º de Dezembro; (282) 402 487; open 9:30am–5:30pm Mon–Fri

Teatro Municipal de Portimão: Largo 1º de Dezembro; open Tue–Sat

Museu de Portimão: Rua D. Carlos I; open Aug: 3–11pm Wed–Sun, 7:30–11pm Tue; Sep–Jul: 10am–6pm Wed–Sun, 2:30–6pm Tue; adm; www.museudeportimao.pt

Igreja do Antigo Colégio da Companhia de Jesus: open 8am–12:30pm & 3:30–5:30pm Mon–Fri

Monumentos Magaliticos de Alcalar: **MAP E5**; Mexilhoeira Grande; (282) 471 410; open Aug: 10am–1pm & 2–6pm Tue–Sat; Sep–July: 10am–1pm & 2–4:30pm Tue–Sat; adm

■ **Sightseeing cruises along the Rio Arade and to the coast depart from the esplanade** ***(see p59)*****.**

■ **The 17th-century Fortaleza da Santa Catarina, at the eastern end of Praia da Rocha, offers fine views.**

■ **For a romantic dinner, book a table at Vista Restaurant** ***(Avenida Tomás Cabreira, Praia da Rocha; www.vistarestaurante.com)*****.**

The Top 10 of Everything

FIESA International Sand Sculpture Festival

Top 10 Moments in History

1 3000 BC: Early People and Trade

Stone burial chambers (dolmens) and menhirs are characteristic of this period. By 1000 BC, the Phoenicians had established sizeable trading stations. The Greeks also arrived, but their trade links were severed by the Carthaginians, who blockaded the Straits of Gibraltar, and in 550 BC founded the city of Portus Hannibalis (Portimão).

Menhir dating from c 3000 BC

2 218–201 BC: Second Punic War

The Romans defeated the Carthaginians, then swept through the Iberian peninsula. During the next 400 years, grand Roman cities and luxurious villas developed.

3 AD 415: Visigoths

After the fall of the Roman Empire, the reins of power were seized by the Visigoths, a formidable warrior caste that came from eastern France and Germany.

4 711: Arrival of the Moors

Internal strife and persecution among the Visigoths ultimately led to one faction appealing for aid from Muslim North Africa. A large army of Berbers and Arabs conquered huge swathes of the Iberian peninsula. The Moors dominated the Algarve for more than 500 years, giving the region its name, al-Gharb, and turning Silves into an intellectual hub of staggering opulence.

5 Christian Crusades

Though Christians reconquered central Portugal in the 12th century, the Algarve was still firmly under Moorish rule. Dom Sancho (1185–1212) briefly took Silves in 1189, but the city was recaptured by Al-Mansur. Dom Sancho II (1223–48) later launched a campaign to invade southern Portugal with the help of northern European Crusaders.

6 Portugal is Born

Faro was the last Moorish stronghold to fall in 1249. Portuguese sovereignty over the Algarve was confirmed in a treaty with the kingdom of Castile in 1297.

7 Maritime Exploration

The Algarve played a pivotal role in Portugal's maritime expansion in the 15th century. Henry the Navigator was made governor of the Algarve in 1418 and initiated the voyages of discovery from his bases in Sagres and Lagos. By the time of his death in 1460, Madeira, the Azores and Cape Verde islands and much of the west coast of Africa had been mapped. In 1488 Bartolomeu Dias sailed to the Cape of Good Hope, and later Vasco da Gama opened the trade route to India.

Painting of Henry the Navigator

Portrait of Portuguese ruler João V

8 Artistic Extravagance

The discovery of gold and diamonds in Brazil during the reign of Pedro II (1683–1706) later financed a period of great artistic extravagance under João V, who ruled Portugal until 1750.

9 Great Earthquake of 1755

The earthquake of 1755 devastated Lisbon and much of southern Portugal and plunged the nation into a long-lasting crisis. Napoleon's troops later invaded in 1807.

Salazar's military coup, 1974

10 Republicanism and Integration with Europe

The late 19th century witnessed political strife, with Republicanism taking root. António de Oliveira Salazar became prime minister in 1932, and turned around a stagnating economy but with the sacrifice of democracy. The army overthrew the government in 1974 in a near-bloodless coup. On 1 January 2002, the country adopted the euro.

MYTHS AND LEGENDS

1 The Moorish King and the Nordic Princess
The mythical king planted thousands of almond trees to convince the princess that the blossom was like the snow she was used to.

2 Henry the Navigator
Henry is said to have assembled the best nautical minds in a prestigious academy, though there is no trace of it today.

3 Curse of the Vixen
On stormy nights, the bellows of a beast can be heard in the hinterland.

4 The Cry of Aben Afen
Listen out for battle cries near Silves – the ghost of the city's last Arab lord.

5 St Vincent
Cabo de São Vicente is associated with a 4th-century martyr, whose body was watched over by 10 ravens.

6 Enchanted Cássima
The pitiful cries of a Moorish woman supposedly echo in the streets close to Loulé Castle.

7 Hannibal and the Elephants
Legend has it that the famous general landed with his troops at Portimão.

8 Manueline Window
King Dom Sebastião (1557–78) is said to have roused an army from the window at Lagos Castle.

9 Pot of Treasure
A pot full of gold coins lies on the road between Mexilhoeira Grande and Praia da Rocha. Kiss the toad guarding it, and the pot is yours.

10 Capture of Aljezur Castle, 1249
A maid might have prevented the capture, but mistook the attacking knights for Moorish defenders and failed to raise the alarm.

Aljezur Castle, captured in 1249

Top 10 Castles and Forts

The battlements of Silves Castle

1 Silves

MAP F4 ■ Open 9am–5:30pm daily (summer: to 7pm) ■ Adm

One of the Algarve's great landmarks, well-preserved Silves Castle dates back to Moorish times, but may have been built on Roman fortifications. Its formidable red sandstone battlements and massive polygonal towers enclose a vast compound.

2 Paderne

MAP G4

The atmospheric ruins of Paderne's long-abandoned Moorish castle are best appreciated on a Sunday morning, or an early evening when the ramparts are illuminated. The thick outer walls of mud and sandstone and the remains of a barbican tower are all that exist of the original structure. Inside, the chapel of Nossa Senhora da Assunção lies in mournful pieces.

Statue of a smuggler, Alcoutim

3 Salir

MAP J3

The ruins of Salir's Moorish castle have been put to novel effect by locals who have sunk gardens in between the battlements and the keep. The rest of the structure can be explored by treading a circular path around the middle of the fortifications. An interesting museum *(see p47)* completes the picture.

4 Alcoutim

Enjoying a lovely setting, Alcoutim *(see p91)* commands glorious views across the River Guadiana to the neighbouring Spanish town of Sanlúcar. The inhabitants of the two settlements were once enemies, but the 14th-century castle was where the short-lived peace treaty between Fernando I and Henrique of Castile was signed on 31 March 1371.

5 Aljezur

MAP C3

Dominating the landscape around Aljezur *(see p101)* are the ruins of the town's 10th-century castle. Perched on a hillock with fabulous views of the coast and Serra de Monchique, this Moorish stronghold controlled an ancient river port and provided a vital link with the open sea. Its broad, overgrown courtyard hides remnants of a vaulted cistern and is surrounded by high ramparts, reinforced by two towers – one round, the other square.

6 Tavira

MAP M4 ■ Open summer: 8:30am–7pm Mon–Fri, 10am–7pm Sat & Sun; winter: 8:30am–5pm Mon–Fri, 9am–5pm Sat & Sun

Only the walls of this old Moorish fortification remain, which surrounds a charming, well-maintained garden. There are lovely views.

7 Fortaleza de Cacela Velha

MAP N4 ■ Closed to public

This pocket-sized fortress sits in the quaint hamlet of Cacela Velha, 8 km (5 miles) west of Monte Gordo, in the eastern Algarve. Polygonal in shape, the building dates from the 18th century and enjoys commanding views over a lagoon that teems with waterfowl. Its squat turrets are topped with whitewashed cones.

8 Fortaleza de Sagres

The fortress is steeped in history and myth, with huge walls and bastions dating from 1793. Little, if anything, remains of Henry the Navigator's original fortress *(see p35)*. Whether or not there was an academy of navigation and astronomy founded here remains a matter of debate and legend. An 18th-century sundial fashioned into the wall is aligned with the famous wind compass, the Rosa dos Ventos.

The view from Fortaleza de Sagres

9 Loulé

MAP J4 ■ Open 9:30am–5:30pm Mon–Fri, 9:30am–2:30pm Sat ■ Adm

Standing on a site *(see pp22–3)* first occupied by the Romans and later by the Moors, the restored battlements here offer splendid views from the ramparts. Dom Afonso III (1210–79) strengthened and expanded the walls of what was a modest military fortification before adding towers and a keep to create a castle.

10 Castelo de Castro Marim

MAP P3 ■ Open Apr–Oct: 9am–7pm daily; Nov–Mar: 9am–5pm ■ Adm

The colossal frontier castle of Castro Marim overlooks the border between Spain and Portugal. Built in the 13th century, the castle was the first headquarters of the Order of Christ. Henry the Navigator was a frequent visitor.

Castelo de Castro Marim

Top 10 Museums

1 Museu Municipal Dr José Formosinho

This highly entertaining ethnographic museum brings together a fantastic collection of oddities, rarities and priceless treasures *(see pp26–9)*.

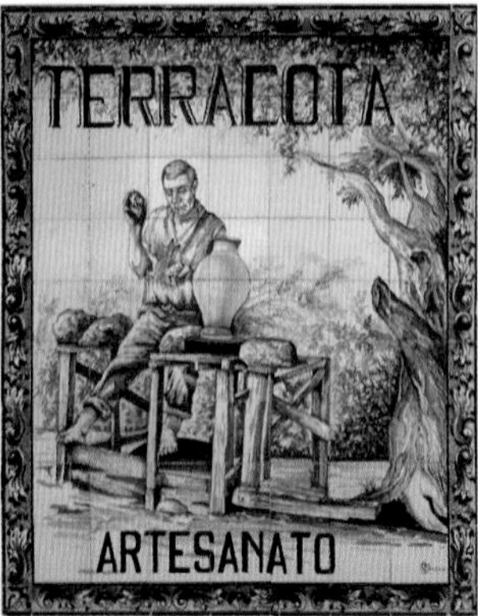

Museu Municipal Dr José Formosinho

2 Museu Municipal de Arqueologia, Silves

This excellent museum *(see pp18–19)* is unique in Portugal for its astonishing 12th-century Arab well-cistern. Unearthed by chance in 1980, it is the star exhibit around which the entire building is constructed. An original staircase, closed to the public and incorporated into the ancient structure, descends 15 m (49 ft) to the bottom of the well. The museum also displays a range of prehistoric, Roman and Moorish antiquities found in Silves.

3 Museu Cerro da Vila, Vilamoura

MAP H5 ■ Cerro da Vila ■ Open May–Oct: 10am–1pm & 4–9pm daily; Nov–Apr: 9:30am–12:30pm & 2–6pm daily ■ Adm

A first-rate modern museum and historic Roman site, Cerro da Vila in Vilamoura is an outstanding example of a 2nd-century villa complex, with sunken baths, salt tanks, a burial tower and brilliant black-and-white-patterned mosaics. The adjacent museum houses a superb display of Roman, Visigoth and Moorish artifacts.

4 Nucleo Islâmico, Tavira

The interior of this absorbing museum *(see pp16–17)* is built around a 12th-century Islamic wall. Among its various exhibits include an inkwell that dates back to the 13th century. There is also a rare eight-handle ceramic pan from the same period. The extraordinary 11th-century "Tavira Vase" is the standout piece.

5 Museu Municipal de Faro

Set within the cloisters of the former convent of Nossa Senhora da Assunção, this museum is one of the Algarve's most beautiful *(see pp12–13)*. It contains a large collection of artifacts and tells the story of Faro's development from Roman times to the present day. Highlights include a giant Roman floor mosaic, fragments of a large Moorish bowl inscribed with "Allah" and a gallery devoted to 16th-century Italian, Spanish and Portuguese paintings.

Museu Municipal de Faro

Exhibit in the Museu de Portimão

6 Museu de Portimão

This superb museum *(see pp38–9)* charts the development of the region's local communities, in particular the fish-canning industry, a former mainstay of the Portuguese economy. Housed in what was once a sardine-canning factory, the museum contains many of the machines used in the industry, and details the processes involved. Other highlights include Roman and Moorish artifacts and the factory's former 19th-century cistern.

7 Museu Municipal de Arqueologia, Albufeira

MAP G5 ■ 1 Praça da República, Albufeira ■ Open 9:30am–5:30pm Tue–Sat ■ Adm

Looking out over the ocean, this modern museum in Albufeira houses a modest but fascinating collection of Stone Age, Roman and Moorish artifacts. The 10th-century Arab silo is worth close scrutiny, as is the set of weathered 16th-century keystones.

8 Pólo Museológico de Salir, Salir

MAP J3 ■ Largo Pedro Dias, Salir ■ (289) 489 137 ■ Open 9am–1pm & 2–5pm Mon–Fri

This museum, housed in the ruins of Salir's Moorish castle *(see pp44–5)*, showcases glazed ceramic bottles and pots dating from the 12th century. Artifacts also include a silver dirham and a funeral tablet inscribed in Arabic. The museum's glass floor is set over an excavated street and remains of dwellings from the time of Islamic occupation. An outdoor platform offers views of the castle walls.

9 Museu Municipal de Loulé

MAP J4 ■ 7 Rua D. Paio Peres Correia ■ Open 9am–6pm Mon–Fri, 9am–2pm Sat ■ Adm (including castle)

Loulé's archaeological heritage is admirably chronicled with displays of Stone Age, Bronze Age and Roman artifacts. Upstairs, history is closer to the present day, with a reconstruction of a traditional Algarve kitchen, replete with 19th-century crockery and a worn *xarém*, or maize wheel.

10 Museu do Traje, São Brás de Alportel

MAP K4 ■ Rua Dr José Dias Sancho ■ (289) 840 100 ■ Open 10am–1pm & 2–5pm Mon–Fri, 2–5pm Sat & Sun ■ Adm

This delightful ensemble of local costumes, decorated carriages and traditional handicrafts is housed in a wonderful country mansion. A particularly poignant exhibit is a child's faded tunic and breeches next to a wonderful photograph of José Maria Féria wearing the same costume in 1929.

Gramophone, Museu do Traje

TOP 10 Beaches

1 Praia do Amado, Carrapateira

Pummelled by Atlantic swells, Amado is one of Portugal's premier surfing venues, and its surf school enjoys international patronage. Sitting well off the beaten track, this west coast beach *(see p102)* also attracts families, and the rock pools at low tide teem with inquisitive children.

2 Praia dos Pescadores, Albufeira

This hugely popular tract of sand *(see p85)* is characterized by the colourful fishing boats stationed at one end – indeed, its name translates as "Fishermen's Beach". Right in front of the town's old quarter, the beach is reached through a tunnel next to the tourist information office.

3 Praia do Camilo, Lagos

Blessed with gorgeous golden sand lapped by crystal clear waters, Camilo's splendour is enhanced by its scenic location. Flanking the beach *(see p102)* are rocky cliffs of a rich ochre hue. Outcrops of mustard-red sandstone lie anchored in the shallows. A nearby warren of secluded coves and hidden grottoes can be explored by boat.

Beautiful Praia do Camilo

Secluded Praia de Odeceixe

4 Praia de Odeceixe

One of the Algarve's best-kept secrets, Odeceixe is in a spectacular setting, up in the northwestern corner of the Algarve. Its sheltered, crescent-shaped beach *(see p102)* is just a short drive (along a road that shadows the path of the river) from the quaint village of Odeceixe. Even in summer, the beach is always wonderfully uncrowded.

5 Praia da Salema, Salema

This select swathe of sand, which lies in front of the fishing village of Salema, is popular with families. The beach also acts as a departure point for some excellent nearby dive

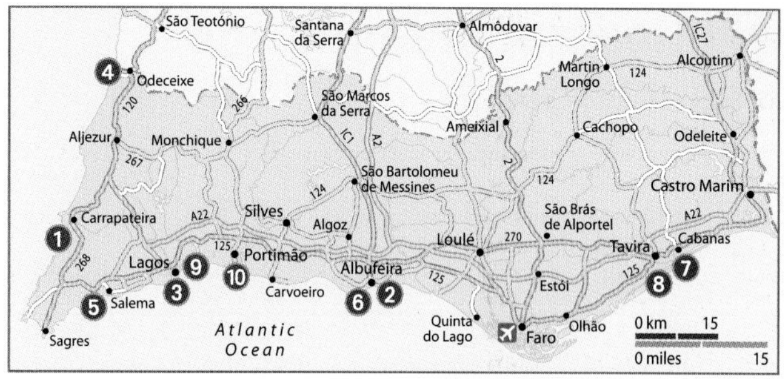

sites, such as Boco do Rio to the east, where the wreck of the *Ocean*, an 18th-century French man-of-war, lies in shallow water, now teeming with fish. Make sure you arrive early to find a parking space.

6 Praia de São Rafael, Albufeira

With its shallow waters and soft white sand, Praia da São Rafael *(see p85)* can fill up quickly. Its pretty bay is framed by some extraordinary rock formations, pitted with a number of caves just waiting to be investigated. It offers ideal snorkelling territory and is popular with families.

7 Praia da Ilha de Cabanas

Reached by ferry, and a favourite with kitesurfers *(see p56)*, the secluded sands on Cabanas beach *(see p94)* stretch for more than 7 km (4 miles).

8 Praia da Ilha de Tavira, Tavira

MAP M5

Ostensibly an elongated sandbar, Ilha de Tavira's windward side is a magnet for enthusiasts of water-sports. Opposite Tavira, the wide, sheltered, sandy beach *(see p94)* skirts a campsite and a string of cafés and fine seafood restaurants. There are two access points to this stretch. From Pedras del Rei, you can walk across a causeway or catch a ride on a miniature rail-way. Alternatively, regular ferry boats depart from the jetty at Quatro Águas.

9 Meia Praia, Lagos

MAP D5

A giant curve of sand, 4 km (2 miles) in length makes this the longest beach *(see p102)* in the Algarve. There is plenty of room for water-skiing, windsurfing and jet-skiing, and for sunbathers seeking a little peace and quiet. It also offers a lovely coastal walk, especially in autumn, when the summer tourists have begun to disperse.

The golden sands of Praia da Rocha

10 Praia da Rocha, Portimão

One of the most famous and impressive beaches in the Algarve, Praia da Rocha *(see p85)* is one vast blanket of golden sand set against a backdrop of cinnamon-coloured cliffs. It can become crowded in summer, but a tunnel at the western end allows access to narrower and often quieter stretches of sand. At various points along Avenida Tómas Cabreira, there is further access via steps – some of which are rather steep.

TOP 10 Coastal Villages and Resort Towns

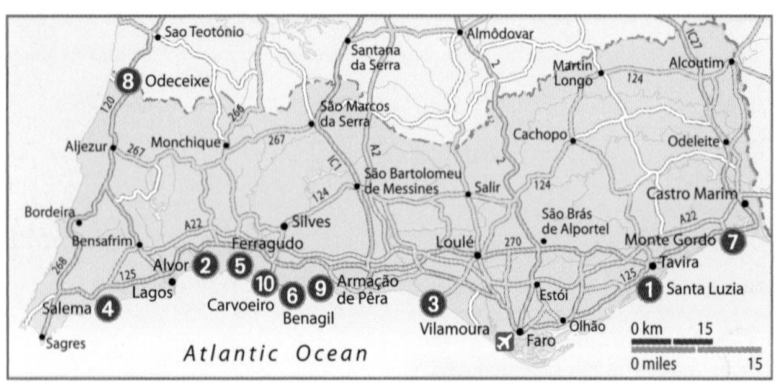

1 Santa Luzia

An old seafaring myth claims Santa Luzia *(see p92)* came by its foreign-sounding name after an effigy of the Virgin Mary was salvaged from an Italian vessel. Today the image most associated with Santa Luzia is *covos* – octopus pots. This is the octopus capital of the Algarve, and hundreds of the earthenware pots can be found piled neatly on the beach in readiness for their next outing.

2 Alvor

MAP D4

Nestling in a sheltered bay midway between Portimão and Lagos, Alvor is an unusual mix of dignified charm and flickering neon. The old quarter is a delight to wander through, the 16th-century Manueline church is stunning and the village restaurants serve some of the tastiest seafood in the region.

Seafood restaurants in Alvor

The glamorous marina in Vilamoura

3 Vilamoura

Designed around a marina of international repute, this upmarket resort has championship golf courses, a stylish casino, luxury hotels and luxurious villas. Fabulous cruises and boat trips to sea caves depart from the marina *(see p83)*.

4 Salema

MAP C5

Even if you are not staying in Salema, it is worth detouring to it from the EN125 via the beautiful ravine, speckled most of the year with colourful flora and fleet-footed goats. The tarmac peters out where the cobbled slip road begins – a causeway cluttered with colourful fishing boats, rickety lobster pots and shrouds of netting. The sloping streets are banked with salt-laced terraced houses and cramped little tavernas.

The picturesque riverfront at Ferragudo

5 Ferragudo

A maze of cottages, converted lofts and cube-like townhouses tumble down towards the river and Praia Grande – a vast swathe of sand popular with sunbathers and windsurfers. The seafood restaurants lining the tidy quayside of this fishing village *(see p83)* are some of the best in the Algarve.

6 Benagil

MAP F5

Benagil straddles a steep, narrow valley, which ambles its way towards a bay the size of a postage stamp. More hamlet than village, Benagil is blessed with a couple of superb seafood restaurants that are positioned on the lip of the valley and offer great views across the ocean.

7 Monte Gordo

MAP P4

A generous sandy beach and a casino (popular with big spenders from Seville) are the twin targets for most visitors here. Monte Gordo is the closest Algarve beach resort to the Spanish border. The esplanade is fringed with lofty palms, and even loftier apartment blocks, with fabulous views of the ocean.

8 Odeceixe

The isolated splendour of this attractive hillside village *(see pp100–101)* makes the long drive north along the Algarve's western coast worthwhile. An old windmill stands at the village's highest point, and is open to visitors in summer. Odeceixe's beach *(see p48)* is sheltered and peaceful, and it is one of the region's most beautiful.

9 Armação de Pêra

MAP F5

The beach here is one of the longest in the Algarve and fronts a commercial hub of tall apartment blocks, seafront hotels and rows of cafés and bars. However this is all rather clinical, so most visitors head east to Pêra's livelier old town which is spread around the site of a small fortress.

The charming town of Carvoeiro

10 Carvoeiro

MAP E5

Friendliness fills this alluring little town, making it ideal for families. It is one of the Algarve's main self-catering areas, and the hilltops that flank the pocket-sized beach are awash with apartments. On the other side of the promontory is the snorkelling territory of Algar Seco rock formation.

Following pages *Praia da Rocha, Portimão*

TOP 10 Inland Villages

1 Salir

The walls of Salir's Moorish castle *(see p44)* are lit up at night and emit an eerie glow, but on the other side of the village *(see p82)* the view is considerably more benign, with vistas stretching across the valley from the parish church and garden. In summer this rural idyll is blanketed by narcissi, and alive with the warbling of brightly coloured passerines.

2 Caldas de Monchique

The warm spa water here has attracted visitors since at least the age of the Roman Empire *(see pp20–21)*. It is just as alluring today, but there are other reasons to visit this hillside hamlet, not least the wood of pine and eucalyptus which provides a lush, cooling canopy in the heat of summer. Woodsmoke and birdsong drift lazily through a valley peppered with whitewashed cottages and smallholdings.

3 Barão de São João

MAP C4

Wrapped in classic hill-walking country and pleasantly lost in time, Barão de São João typifies rural Algarve. It is perhaps best appreciated during the antiques fair, which the village hosts on the last Sunday of every month.

The church in Querença

4 Querença

Surrounded by the rugged Caldeirão mountains, Querença *(see p84)* is relatively isolated, which is part of its allure. It is best known for its 16th-century church and the ancient, weather-worn cross that stands at the southern edge of the village's picturesque square.

5 Estói

Just off the town's *(see p93)* main square is the Palácio do Visconde de Estói, a restored 19th-century Rococo palace (now a beautiful *pousada*), with gardens fanned by giant palms and cooled by fountains. A 20-minute walk from here brings you to Milreu, the

Palácio do Visconde de Estói

remains of a grand Roman villa. The site is dominated by the apse of a temple that was converted into a Christian basilica in the 5th century. The baths, complete with fish mosaics, are another highlight.

6 Alcoutim

The town's *(see p91)* 14th-century castle keeps one timeworn eye on its townsfolk and the other on the old adversary, Sanlúcar, Alcoutim's mirror image on the Spanish side of the River Guadiana. Served by a small ferry, the two villages in different countries are also connected by the only cross-border zip line in the world (www.limitezero.com).

7 Paderne

Early in the 17th century the entire population of Paderne *(see p84)* moved from the shadows of the nearby castle to the environs of a newly consecrated church. That village is now a sleepy place of faded charm and modest means, but therein lies its beauty. The architecture retains a certain grandeur, while the Moorish castle stands close by, perhaps still wondering where all the people went.

8 Guerreiros do Rio

MAP P2

The scenic road south from Alcoutim runs partly along the banks of the River Guadiana and passes through a landscape bristling with olive, fig and carob trees before reaching this tiny village. Amid the orange trees, a former schoolhouse now contains a modest museum that provides a glimpse into the history of the river.

9 Martim Longo

MAP L1 ■ Workshop: 9am–noon Mon–Fri except public hols

The storks nesting on top of the belfry of Martim Longo's parish church have been members of this small community for years, and they are as appealing as their unusual home. The "A Flor da Agulha" dolls' workshop is also worth a visit for its traditional, hand-crafted jute dolls.

A cobbled street in Alte

10 Alte

The village's cobbled streets, colourful window frames and cheerful chimney pots invoke an unhurried air that is quite disarming. Alte's *(see p82)* charming church, situated near a leafy square, retains a fine entrance. The spring running along its flank tumbles under an old mill, providing a great picnic spot.

TOP 10 Outdoor Pursuits

Kayaking around the unusual rock formations at Praia da Piedade, Lagos

1 Diving

MAP E5 ■ Ocean Revival Park: www.oceanrevival.org

Some wonderful dive sites are found on the Algarve's southwestern coast. The Ocean Revival Park *(see p39)* is an artificial reef composed of four decommissioned navy warships.

2 Cycling and Mountain Biking

MAP K3 ■ Lisa Bikes: www.lisabikes.com

A great way to explore the Algarve is by renting a bicycle. Lisa Bikes arranges self-guided or guided tours, and several mountain-bike adventure companies run cross-country rides.

Cycling near Faro

3 Kayaking

MAP D5 ■ Extreme Algarve: Lagos; www.extremealgarve.com

The Alvor and Ria Formosa estuaries are perfect for kayaking. Discover the sea caves at Ponta da Piedade *(see p26)* with Extreme Algarve.

4 Birdwatching

MAP B5 ■ SPEA: www.spea.pt

Numerous birds are attracted to the Sagres peninsula, Serra de Monchique and Ria Formosa Estuary. The Society for the Study of Birds (SPEA) website has a page devoted to birding tourism (www.birdlife.org).

5 Kite Surfing

MAP N4 ■ Kite Surf Eolis: www.kitesurfeolis.com

Wind conditions off the beaches near Tavira *(see p94)* are particularly good for beginners in kitesurfing. The lagoons around Alvor *(see p50)* are best suited to the more experienced.

6 Big Game Fishing

MAP D5 ■ Blue Shark: Lagos Marina; (916) 788 552; www.blueshark.pt

The Algarve has a long history of fishing, and the warm coastal waters still attract marlin and sharks between June and September. Some operators such as Blue Shark practise a tag and release policy.

7 Ancient Archaeology Tour

MAP B5 ■ Menhir circuit, Hortas do Tabual, Vila do Bispo

Follow a signposted circuit around 5,000-year-old menhirs near the village of Vila do Bispo *(see p101)*.

8 Zip Wire

MAP P1 ■ Limitezero: Sanlúcar de Guadiana; www.limitezero.com

The world's first cross-border zip line ride is a 720-metre cable rigged between the villages of Alcoutim *(see p91)* and Sanlúcar in Spain.

Surfing the Atlantic waves

9 Surfing

MAP C3 ■ Algarve Surf School: www.algarvesurfschool.com

Algarve's Atlantic rollers provide the perfect conditions for surfing and bodyboarding. Algarve Surf School is one of many excellent camps.

10 Horse Riding

MAP J5 ■ Pinetrees Riding Centre: Corgo da Zorra; (289) 394 369; www.pinetrees.pt

Northwest of Lagos and around Silves is idyllic horse riding territory. Pinetrees Centre offers riding in the Parque Natural da Ria Formosa.

Horse riding in the Algarve

TOP 10 ALGARVE SURF SCHOOLS

Surfing lessons on the beach

1 Extreme Algarve
This highly reputed surf school offers quick refreshers and intensive courses (www.extremealgarve.com).

2 Algarve Surf Shop & School
An Algarvian institution since 1966, this surf school in Sagres caters for all levels (www.algarvesurfschool.com).

3 Jah Shaka Surf Shop
Rent a board for a day or try out kitesurfing, stand up paddle and daily yoga classes (jahshakasurf.com).

4 Albufeira Surf & SUP
Learn how to surf, stand-up paddle board, cliff jump, and explore the coast by Kayak (albufeirasurfsup.com).

5 Future Surfing School
This surf school is located at one of the Algarve's most beautiful beaches, the stunning Praia da Rocha in Portimão (www.future-surf.com).

6 SW Surf Shop
Learn with the locals in the fishing village of Aljezur in the northwest Algarve (swsurfshop.com).

7 Arrifana Surf School and Camp
Located on Arrifana Beach, this school promises great surf in a spectacular setting (arrifanasurfschool.com).

8 Wavy Surf Camp
Experience the Algarve's incredible surf in style at this luxury surf camp in Sagres (www.wavysurfcamp.com).

9 Fil Surf School
Fil Surf School shuttles students of all ages to and from the pristine Monte Clerigo beach (www.filsurf.com).

10 Wavesensations Sagres
Wavesensations offers lessons for adults and kids from age 6 and up (wavesensations.com).

TOP 10 Coastal and River Cruises

1 Santa Bernarda Pirate Ship

MAP E4 ■ Rua Júdice Fialho 11, Portimão ■ (967) 023 840 ■ Open Feb–Nov: Mon–Sat ■ www.santa-bernarda.com

Discover caves and coves, before enjoying a beach barbecue, on the exciting themed cruises and special expeditions aboard this pirate ship.

The Santa Bernarda Pirate Ship

2 Rio Sul Guadiana

MAP P4 ■ Rua Tristão Vaz Teixeira 15, Monte Gordo ■ (281) 510 200 ■ Open every Tue, Thu (& Sun May–Oct) ■ www.riosultravel.com

A trip along the Guadiana, passing the Reserva Natural do Sapal. Have lunch at Foz de Odeleite and enjoy music and wine on your return.

3 Bom Dia

MAP D5 ■ Marina de Lagos 10 ■ (282) 087 587 ■ Open mid-Mar–Nov ■ www.bomdia-boattrips.com

The colourful Bom Dia schooner sets sail from Lagos harbour for the Ponte de Piedade grottoes, where dinghies allow closer inspection of these natural wonders.

4 Ilha Deserta Cruise

MAP K6 ■ Porta Nova Wharf, Faro ■ (918) 779 155 ■ www.animaris.pt

A maritime expedition through the waterways of the Parque Natural da Ria Formosa is possibly the best way in which to explore this diverse wetland. Lunch is at O Estaminé, which specializes in seafood.

5 Dream Wave

MAP G5 ■ Lote 5, Loja 21, Marina de Albufeira ■ (962) 003 885/801 ■ www.dreamwavealgarve.com

Enjoy a leisurely cruise on the Leãozinho sailboat, or experience an adrenaline rush on the powerful and rapid Jet Boat or Ocean Rocket.

6 Condor de Vilamoura

MAP H5 ■ Cais I 25, Marina de Vilamoura ■ (961) 401 141 ■ Open mid-Mar–Oct ■ www.condordevilamoura.com

Choose between a trip to Albufeira's coastal grottoes or a cruise with a beach barbecue at Armação de Pêra.

The Bom Dia, moored at Lagos Harbour

Boat trip on the Rio Arade

7 Rio Arade

MAP E4 ■ Esplanade, Portimão ■ (966) 807 621 ■ www.alvorboattrips.com

This ancient waterway provides an absorbing journey to Silves *(see pp18–19)*, where you can explore for an hour before returning.

8 Seafaris

MAP D5 ■ Seafari Stand, Marina de Lagos ■ (282) 798 727 ■ Hours vary seasonally ■ www.seafaris.net

Claiming sightings on 80 per cent of its journeys, this semi-inflatable powers out of the marina. When dolphins are seen, it reduces speed and waits for a display of their antics.

Seagulls on the Ria Formosa

9 Ria Formosa

MAP K6 ■ Marina de Faro ■ (918) 720 002 ■ www.formosamar.com

Traditional fishing boats take you through the channels and lagoons of the Parque Natural *(see pp30–33)*.

10 San Lorenzo Champagne Cruises

MAP H5 ■ Marina de Vilamoura ■ (965) 656 675 ■ www.boatcharteralgarve.com

Enjoy a flute of champagne as you step aboard this luxury motor yacht and cruise around in style.

TOP 10 ALGARVE COASTAL AND WETLAND BIRD SPECIES

1 Greater Flamingo
A common resident of the Castro Marim and Ria Formosa areas, especially during the winter.

2 Collared Pratincole
A summer migrant, this wading bird appears in coastal wetlands, particularly the Castro Marim marshes.

3 Audouin's Gull
A large gull distinguished by its stubby red bill. Although present all year, its numbers swell in winter.

4 Spoonbill
A long-legged wading bird seen in coastal lagoons all year, but especially abundant in winter.

5 Caspian Tern
The Alvor estuary and Castro Marim marshes are favourite winter habitats for the world's largest tern.

6 Kentish Plover
A ubiquitous shorebird present all year, it is very easy to observe along the Ria Formosa and Alvor estuaries.

7 Black-winged Kite
Winter is the best time to spot this sleek raptor. Habitats include the Vilamoura reed beds.

8 Red-rumped Swallow
The Arade and Guadiana riverbanks are the preferred nesting sites for this handsome summer species.

9 Glossy Ibis
Its shiny reddish-brown body and bottle-green wings lend this winter wader its name.

10 Black-winged Stilt
Arguably the most symbolic of resident Algarvean waders; its habitats include the wetlands near Faro.

A black-winged stilt in wetlands

Top 10 Golf Courses

Penina Academy golf course

1 Penina Academy Course

MAP E4 ■ Penina Hotel & Golf Resort, Penina, near Portimão ■ www.penina.com

A compact, 9-hole course laid out amid the Championship fairways, the ease of play here should relax even the most nervous of players. The adjoining golf academy offers individual or group tuition.

2 Royal Course, Vale do Lobo

MAP J5 ■ Royal Golf Course, Vale do Lobo ■ www.valedolobo.com

A rolling terrain abundant with pine envelopes this par 72 layout. The highlight is the infamous 16th, where a powerful and accurate swing is needed to carry a set of precipitous cliffs before the green. The signature hole is the 9th, with its spectacular, semi-island green.

3 San Lorenzo

In the Parque Natural da Ria Formosa, and one of the top five golf courses in continental Europe, the par 72 layout culminates with a green on the 18th that must be approached from across a lake. Part of the Dona Filipa & San Lorenzo Golf Resort *(see p127)*, the course *(see p86)* is open to visitors, with priority given to hotel guests. The clubhouse restaurant has a lovely terrace with views over the greens.

4 Pine Cliffs

With a clifftop layout, this 9-hole golf course *(see p86)* is set against an ocean backdrop and offers spectacular views. The course hides under a canopy of umbrella pine, with narrow fairways demanding a steady swing. The final hole requires a shot from the "Devil's Parlour" clifftop tee that will carry a deep ravine to hit the green.

5 Victoria

MAP H5 ■ Anantara Vilamoura Algarve Resort ■ www.anantara.com/en/vilamoura-algarve

Designed by golf legend Arnold Palmer, this undulating 18-hole par 72 layout is regarded as one of the best and most sophisticated courses in Europe. It features wide fairways and extensive water hazards.

Royal Course, Vale do Lobo

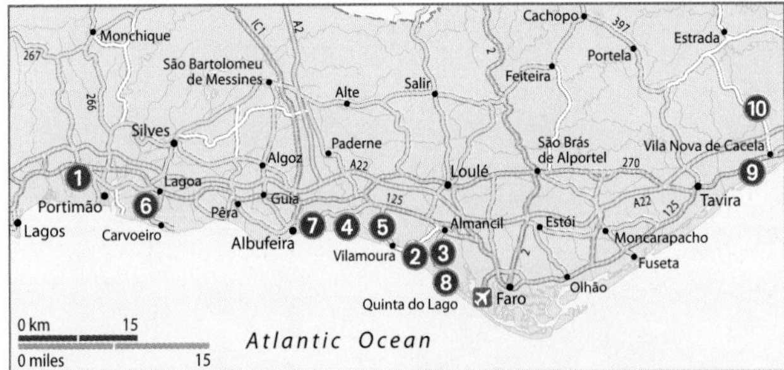

6 Gramacho Course, Pestana Carvoeiro

MAP E5 ▪ Pestana Golf & Resort, Carvoeiro ▪ www.pestanagolf.com

Gramacho gained another 9-hole layout to add to the original double 9, and the combination allows for a variety of options in pin settings and length to suit those with a high or a low handicap.

7 Balaia

Popular with beginners, as well as with the more adroit, this layout *(see p86)* is recommended for the holiday golfer who prefers a fairly relaxed game. It still requires a degree of concentration, however, especially when it comes to club selection, as the holes vary in length more than one might expect in a 9-hole course.

8 Quinta do Lago South

This par 72 championship course *(see p86)* within the estate of the same name has hosted the Portuguese Open on several occasions, and is one of the flagship European Tour courses. The undulating layout favours long hitters, but strategic bunkering, the odd water hazard and large, contoured greens provide plenty of challenges. Despite its championship status, the course welcomes golfers of all abilities, and has two well-equipped clubhouses.

9 Quinta da Ria

MAP N4 ▪ Quinta da Ria, near Vila Nova de Cacela ▪ www.quintadaria.com

Bordering the Parque Natural da Ria Formosa *(see pp30–33)*, this 18-hole par 72 layout golf course is said to be one of the best in the region and offers great ocean views. The five lakes were built to provide natural obstacles in the course of the game and also to support the flora and fauna. The many carob, olive and almond trees are now home to numerous species.

The 18-hole Quinta da Ria golf course

10 Monte Rei

MAP N4 ▪ Monte Rei Golf & Country Club, Sesmarias ▪ www.monte-rei.com

The celebrated Jack Nicklaus designed this par 72 championship course, part of an upmarket country club located behind Vila Nova de Cacela. The layout is known for its ingeniously shaped bunkers and challenging water hazards. Facilities include a plush clubhouse and a highly regarded golf academy.

TOP 10 Children's Attractions

The Almancil Karting circuit

1 Almancil Karting

MAP J5 ■ Vale d'Éguas, Almancil ■ Open 2–7pm Tue, 10am–7pm Wed–Sun (hours may vary according to seasons) ■ Adm ■ www.kartingalgarve.com

Experience life in the fast lane at this challenging circuit, catering for everyone. Two-seater karts (for an adult and child to ride together) and karts adapted for people with reduced mobility are available.

2 Parque da Mina

MAP E3 ■ Sítio do Vale de Boi, Caldas de Monchique ■ Open Oct–Mar: 10am–5pm; Apr–Sep: 10am–7pm; closed Nov–Mar: Mon & Tue ■ Adm ■ www.parquedamina.com

An adventure theme park, complete with a playground and heritage centre. With advanced booking, the energetic may traverse a lofty rope slide. Visitors can try and find their way out of a mirror maze, the park's latest attraction.

3 Krazy World Zoo

MAP G4 ■ Lagoa de Viseu, near Algoz ■ Open 10am–6pm daily (Jul & Aug: to 6:30pm; winter hours vary) ■ Adm ■ www.krazyworld.com

Snakes and alligators are among the residents at this animal park. The pet farm is sanctuary to smaller, more cuddly creatures. Children can enjoy pony rides, play a round of mini-golf or have fun in the inflatable playground.

4 Zoomarine

MAP G5 ■ Estrada Nacional 125, Guia ■ Open mid-Mar–Oct: 10am–6pm daily (Jul & Aug: to 7:30pm) ■ Adm ■ www.zoomarine.pt

This popular marine park is one of the Algarve's top attractions. Promoting conservation and environmental education, Zoomarine is home to dolphins, seals, sea lions, a variety of tropical birds and marine species. Complete with water slides, a wave pool and 4D cinema, there's plenty here to entertain kids and grown-ups.

Visitors having fun at Zoomarine

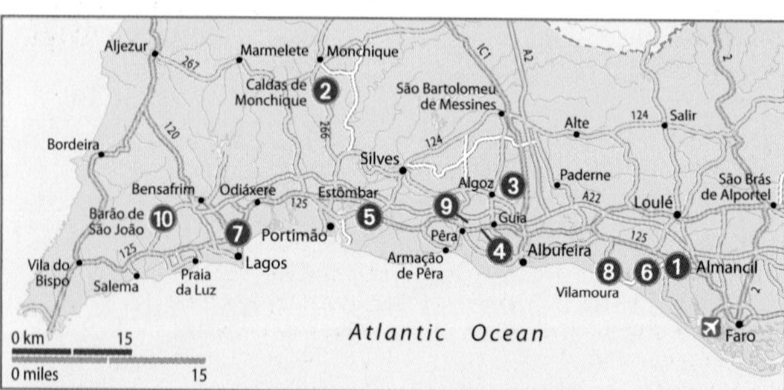

***Previous pages** Staircase decorated with tiles, Pousada Palácio de Estói*

Children enjoying some of the attractions at Slide & Splash

5 Slide & Splash

MAP E4 ■ Estrada 125, Vale de Deus, Estômbar, near Lagoa ■ Open Apr–Oct: 10am–5:30pm daily (summer: to 6pm); closed Apr & Oct: Sun ■ Adm ■ www.slidesplash.com

Corkscrew, Disco River and the Big Wave are some of the best water chutes at this fun waterpark. The adrenaline rush starts working overtime when you are halfway down the Banzai water slide.

6 Aquashow Family Park

MAP H5 ■ Semino, near Quarteira ■ Open May–Sep: daily ■ Adm ■ www.aquashowpark.com

The Free Fall water slide at this theme park is the only one of its kind in Europe and is a ride to remember. Other favourites are the White Fall, Water Coaster and Wild Snake water chutes, which the biggest in Europe. Toddlers can paddle in Aqualand – the playground is in the swimming pool.

7 Lagos Adventure Park

MAP D5 ■ Albardeira, Meia Praia, Lagos ■ Opening times vary (depends on weather) ■ Adm ■ www.lusoaventura.com

With high rope courses of varying difficulty levels, set in the trees of a pine forest near the beach, this park offers adventure and entertainment for all. Participants move through a series of obstacles as they make their way through "cobwebs", climb vertical nets and traverse numerous rope ladders. Other exciting activities, such as paintball, are also on offer.

8 Family Golf Park

MAP H5 ■ Rua dos Marmeleiros, Vilamoura ■ (289) 300 800 ■ Open Feb–Nov: from 10am daily (closing times vary) ■ Adm ■ www.familygolfpark.pt

A great attraction for the whole family, where two 18-hole mini-golf courses test the skills of both children and parents. Catch the tourist train that tours Vilamoura before returning for refreshments at the café.

9 FIESA International Sand Sculpture Festival

MAP F4 ■ Between Pêra and Algoz ■ Open Mar, Sep & Nov: 10am–7pm daily; Jun & Jul: 10am–10pm daily ■ Closing times vary ■ Adm ■ www.fiesa.org

The Algarve's international sand sculpture festival brings together some of the world's most talented artists. The huge sculptures are illuminated at night.

10 Lagos Zoological Park

MAP D4 ■ Estrada Municipal de Bensafrim, Barão de S. João ■ Open 10am–5pm daily (summer: to 7pm) ■ Adm ■ www.zoolagos.com

Lemurs, gibbons and Vietnamese pigs share the grounds with graceful flamingoes, leggy emus, toucans and bouncing wallabies. The lynxes are a highlight.

Flamingo at Lagos Zoo

TOP 10 Walks and Hikes

1 Via Algarviana

MAP P1–B5 ■ Alcoutim to Cabo de São Vicente

The greatest of all Algarve hiking trails, the epic GR13 crosses the region from Alcoutim in the east to the western tip of Portugal. With several scenic connected trails, this 300-km (186-mile) route takes around ten days to complete and mostly heads through mountains and woodlands before meeting the coast at the end.

Sunset at Praia de Odeceixe

2 Odeceixe Loop

MAP C2 ■ Odeceixe Beach loop

This easy 13-km (8-mile) walk begins at Odeceixe and follows the River Seixe to the Atlantic where the incredible Praia de Odeceixe is the ideal place to relax. From there, the trail heads south across coastal cliffs before turning inland and passing through agricultural land back to Odeceixe.

3 Rocha da Pena Trail

MAP H3 ■ Rocha da Pena loop

In the mountains north of Albufeira, this 6.4-km (4-mile) signposted circular route from the village of Rocha da Pena follows rocky footpaths surrounded by varied flora up to almost 500 m (1,600 ft) above sea level. If tackling the route on a hot day remember to bring plenty of water.

4 Don Quixote Trail

MAP L2 ■ Casas Baixas

In the remote east of the Algarve, this diverse loop starts at the Discovery Centre in the village of Casa Baixas, and over the next 17 km (10.5 miles) passes through forests of cork-oak and pine, follows streams across floodplains and climbs mountains, with ample fauna to spot as you go. The trail takes its name from the windmills that hikers pass on the route.

5 Ladeiras do Pontal Trail

MAP P2 ■ Miradouro do Pontal

Signposted PR2, this circular route follows dirt roads and rocky paths over hills and valleys to the River Guadiana that forms the border between Portugal and Spain, which you can peer over from various viewpoints along the route. This 13.5-km (8-mile) trail can be very dry and provides little shade, so it is best tackled outside the height of summer.

6 Ilha da Culatra Trail

MAP L6 ■ Ferry landing, Culatra

Culatra, an island off the south coast, is a short ferry ride from Olhão. This easy trail, just 5.6 km (3.5 miles) long, passes through raised timber walkways, sandy beaches and dunes. This route is the perfect way to explore the island's beauty and is particularly popular among those looking to spot birds and sea life.

7 Serra do Caldeirão

MAP L4 ■ Parises

The hills and mountains north of Faro are great for walking and are easily accessible from the coast. This 20-km- (12.5-mile-) long, sign-posted figure of eight is a diverse hike, traversing mountain streams, rocky passes and various types of woodland as well as visiting a couple of remote villages along the way. It's a long day so make sure you take enough food and water with you.

8 Albufeira to Alte Link

MAP G5–H3 ■ Albufeira Tourist Office to Ribeira de Alte

A 29-km (18-mile) uphill slog, this trail, which connects to the Via Algarviana, passes through the Barrocal, the region between the coast and the mountains further inland. Here, there are many rock formations of irregular shape known as "barrocos". There are food stops along the way. Try for an early start to make the most of this scenic trail and the best time to attempt this long day hike is spring.

Visitors taking in the views at Fóia

9 Fóia Trail

MAP E3 ■ Fóia

Passing through the eucalyptus forests of the Serra de Monchique, this 7-km (4.5-mile) mountain circuit takes you right up into the Algarve's hinterland. Reaching almost 900 m (2,950 ft) above sea level, it passes plenty of plant species along the way and provides panoramic views of the coast. The trail is well signposted.

10 Seven Hanging Valleys Trail

MAP E5–H5 ■ Marinha Beach loop

Traversing through deep valleys carved out by rivers, this circular hike near Lagoa crosses seven valleys along the coast, each offering scenic views along the 12-km (7.5-mile) trail. Several beaches on the way provide perfect spots for picnic and swimming. The trail ends at Praia do Centeanes.

Hikers exploring the Seven Hanging Valleys Trail

TOP 10 Culinary Highlights of the Algarve

1 Sardinhas Assadas

The humble and ubiquitous sardine is arguably the most popular menu choice in the region. Bursting with goodness, sardines are at their plumpest during summer, and are simply mouth-watering when charcoal-grilled and served with boiled potatoes and salad.

***Sardinhas assadas*, a popular dish**

2 Amêijoas na Cataplana

If there is one dish synonymous with the Algarve's rich ocean harvest, it's this one. Fresh cockles are sealed in a *cataplana*, a rounded copper cooking vessel resembling a wok. Allowed to cook in their own steam with a combination of *presunto* (cured ham), *chouriço* (sausage), tomato, lemon, olive oil and garnished with coriander and garlic, the result is a succulent seafood delight. It is best enjoyed with chilled white wine.

Delicious *amêijoas na cataplana*

Classic *porco à Alentejana*

3 Porco à Alentejana

This intrepid marriage of pork and clams appears to bring the ocean and the countryside together, although it's a feast that originated in the vast plains of the Alentejo. The ingredients are cooked in a spicy marinade of white wine, fresh garlic and paprika. If the dish is prepared correctly, the shells should be open when served.

4 Arroz de Polvo

A regional speciality which again evokes the Algarve's love affair with the sea. Tender morsels of fresh octopus are added to a mix of fried onion and parsley, and then gently boiled with wine vinegar and a dash of chilli powder. Rice is added, with salt and pepper to taste. The meal is usually served with a side dish of black olives and generous slices of crusty bread.

5 Doces de Amêndoa

Almonds (another Moorish import) are used to make these colourful little delicacies that can look like fish, fruit, birds, smiling faces and even vegetable baskets.

6 Cabrito Assado

Roasted kid is one of the gastronomical wonders of the rural Algarve. The meat is brushed with a thin layer of lard, sprinkled with minced bacon and laced with white wine. Garnished with whole garlic cloves and dusted with paprika, it is slowly roasted until crispy brown.

7 Gaspacho do Algarve

This version of gazpacho soup differs from its well-known Spanish counterpart in that the ingredients are not pulverized, enabling it to retain a delightfully crunchy texture. Served cold, this heavenly blend of tomato, garlic, cucumber, oregano and sweet pepper sprinkled with diced crouton is bliss on a hot day.

8 Bifes de Atum

The livelihoods of whole communities used to depend on tuna. It is not fished so hard now, but is still a favourite in thousands of restaurants along the coast. Try *atum de cebola*, a tasty blend of melted butter and tomato sauce with onions, garlic and parsley, poured over a firm tuna steak garnished with lemon wedges.

9 Morgado de Figo

Figs were introduced by the Moors and soon became an integral part of the Algarve's cuisine. Fig lord cakes are dainty creations moulded from a fig-and-almond paste.

Frango assado com piri-piri

10 Frango Assado com Piri-Piri

The great Portuguese standby: some restaurants in the Algarve serve nothing else. Generous platters of juicy chicken portions are served with crisp French fries and green-pepper salad. The meat comes with optional red chilli sauce, which is homemade and usually hot.

TOP 10 ALGARVE WINES, LIQUEURS AND SPIRITS

Bottles of Medronho

1 Medronho
The celebrated *aguardente* (brandy) is produced commercially, but the best is the "Monchique Moonshine", which is distilled by locals in their homes.

2 Tapada da Torre
The flagship label *(see p87)* from local winemaker João O'Neill Mendes. Both red and white are exceptionally smooth on the palate.

3 Quê
A sparkling rosé made at the Barranco Longo vineyard from the *touriga nacional* grape.

4 Vida Nova
Wine produced from Sir Cliff Richard's Algarve estate *(see p72)*. With a rich, spicy bouquet, this red sings of young berry fruit.

5 Amarguinha
A sweet bitter-almond liqueur from the Algarve. It is ideal as an apéritif or as a digestif.

6 Barranco Longo
The Reserva Red is produced from *touriga nacional* and *syrah* grapes.

7 Aperitivo Algarseco
An underrated Algarvian dry white apéritif wine, which is similar to an amontillado.

8 Licor de Tangerina
Wonderfully fragrant liqueur with the tang of lush citrus groves.

9 Brandy-mel
A potent mix of brandy and honey, this is a favourite mid-winter tipple.

10 Odelouca River Valley
Expressive, elegant and very well-balanced red wine from the Quinta do Francês winery *(see p72)*.

TOP 10 Restaurants

Atmospheric terrace at Casa Velha

1 Casa Velha, Quinta do Lago

French haute cuisine is served in this 300-year-old converted farmhouse *(see p89)*, with an attractive outdoor terrace. With more than 200 Portuguese red wines to choose from, it will appeal to wine connoisseurs and seasoned gourmets alike. Dishes served include the Marbré of Duck Foie Gras with figs and the King Crab with Ossetra Caviar.

2 Brisa do Rio, Tavira

This friendly backstreet eatery *(see p95)* has received glowing praise for its outstanding regional fare, such as black pork *cataplana* (casserole) with clams. An outdoor seating area is also available.

3 O Barradas, Silves

Set in a converted country farmhouse, this restaurant *(see p89)* has a comfortable indoor seating area, complete with a fireplace. It also offers guests the option to dine outside in the garden, or on the covered terrace. The dishes served here are modern takes on traditonal Portuguese cuisine. Culinary highlights include baked wild fish and the *Mirandesa* (veal served with fig chutney).

4 Adega Vila Lisa, Mexilhoeira Grande

Renowned Portuguese food critic José Quitério regards this charming rural eatery *(see p105)* as one of the best in the country. The five-course tasting menu features traditional dishes such as *canja de conquilhas* (cockle broth), but it changes daily, depending on what's fresh and available. Make sure you book well in advance as the restaurant is very popular, particularly in peak season.

5 O Terraço, Martinhal

Traditional Portuguese cuisine is offered with flair and imagination at this contemporary restaurant *(see p105)*. Serving hotel and resort guests, as well as non-residents, the emphasis is family-oriented, and the menu will appeal to both refined tastes and young palates.

6 Mirandus, Lagos

This enchanting gourmet restaurant *(see p105)* is perched on the top of a cliff with stunning views out to sea. You can choose from a five-course set menu, which changes every day, or make your selections à la carte. The menu is put together by the resident chef, and specially

Stunning views from the Mirandus

focuses on fresh seasonal and local produce. Vegetarian and vegan options are available alongside authentic meat and fish dishes. The wine list is an inspiration in itself. Be sure to book in advance.

Waterfront views at Sueste

7 Sueste, Ferragudo

The bizarre-looking but incredibly tasty *imperador* (emperor fish) is one of the more unusual treats on offer at this fabulous quayside restaurant *(see p89)* overlooking the River Arade. Spectacular summer sunsets bathe the terrace with a golden light, adding greatly to Sueste's appeal. Seafood dominates the menu, and you can watch the chef grilling the catch of the day by the waterfront.

8 Ocean, Alporchinhos

MAP F5 ■ Vila Vita Parc, Rua Anneliese Pohl, Alporchinhos ■ (282) 310 100 ■ Closed Tue ■ Reservations required ■ No veg dishes ■ www.restauranteocean.com ■ €€€

Dishes such as red mullet, Spello beans and Andalusian prawn have earned chef Hans Neuner and his team two Michelin stars. The international wine list is excellent.

9 Veneza, Paderne

A warm atmosphere pervades this exceptional family-run restaurant *(see p89)*. The traditional cuisine is straight out of grandma's kitchen – hearty country fare prepared from hand-me-down recipes. The award-winning wine cellar heaves with more than 1,000 labels which are all stored under excellent conditions.

10 Vila Joya, Albufeira

An exclusive gourmet restaurant, the Villa Joya *(see p89)* has two Michelin stars to its name. Austrian chef Dieter Koschina's inventive take on traditional Portuguese cuisine uses northern European techniques. Experienced sommeliers help in pairing the excellent dishes with the best wines.

Pretty poolside setting at Vila Joya

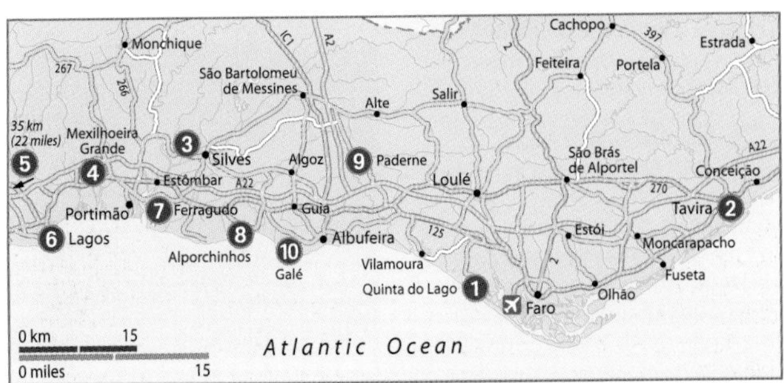

TOP 10 Wineries

1 Quinta do Francês

MAP E4 ▪ Sítio da Dobra, Odelouca ▪ (282) 106 303 ▪ Open mid-Mar–mid-Nov: 10am–1pm & 2–5:30pm Tue–Sun; mid-Nov–mid-Mar: 10am–1pm & 2–5:30pm Mon–Fri ▪ Advance booking for groups ▪ www.quintadofrances.com

Wines from here *(see p19)* are found in some of the Algarve's finest restaurants, and have an international reputation. Tastings are hosted in the wine shop where you can buy the flagship, Quinta do Francês Syrah red.

Quinta do Francês wine shop

2 Quinta do Barradas

MAP F4 ▪ Sítio da Venda Nova, near Silves ▪ (282) 443 308 ▪ Open 3–6pm Thu–Tue ▪ Advance booking required ▪ www.obarradas.com

Cultivated by the same team that runs O Barradas restaurant *(see p89)*, the vineyard is a complementary venture that has resulted in some fruity and exuberant wines, notably the Quinta do Barradas Selecção. Tours take in the winery and a boutique wine store. The wines produced on the property are, of course, stocked in the restaurant's cellar.

3 Quinta dos Vales

MAP E4 ▪ Sítio dos Vales, near Estombar ▪ (282) 431 036 ▪ Open 9am–1pm & 2–6pm Mon–Fri (summer: to 7pm daily) ▪ Guided wine tasting and tour: advanced booking required ▪ www.quintadosvales.eu

One of the region's leading producers, this verdant estate is renowned for its many award-winning wines, among them the celebrated Marquês dos Vales Grace Touriga-Nacional. Besides the winery, tours take in extensive gardens where colourful and quirky sculpture is exhibited. Visitors can also take part in art workshops. On-site accommodation is available for those wishing to linger.

4 Quinta da Vinha

MAP F4 ▪ Sítio da Vala, near Lagoa ▪ (912) 104 557 ▪ Open 9am–6pm Mon–Fri ▪ Advance booking required ▪ www.josemanuelcabrita.wix.com/quintadavinha

Despite basic amenities, this winery is worth investigating for its delightfully understated appeal that belies the quality of the wines produced. Visitors can taste three different wines – red, white and rosé – served with a delicious selection of hams, cheeses and smoked sausage. The Cabrita Reserva 2014, an "intense and heavenly" red, is a must-have bottle to take away.

5 Adega do Cantor

MAP G4 ▪ Quinta do Miradouro, Guia ▪ (968) 776 971 ▪ Open 10am–1pm & 2–5pm daily ▪ Guided tours: advance booking required ▪ www.winesvidanova.com

Sir Cliff Richard is the celebrity name behind the "Winery of the Singer" – the vineyard is on his property near Albufeira. After a tour visitors can taste wines from the Vida Nova and Onda Nova range. An open-air terrace overlooks one of the vineyards.

Lovely views at Adega do Cantor

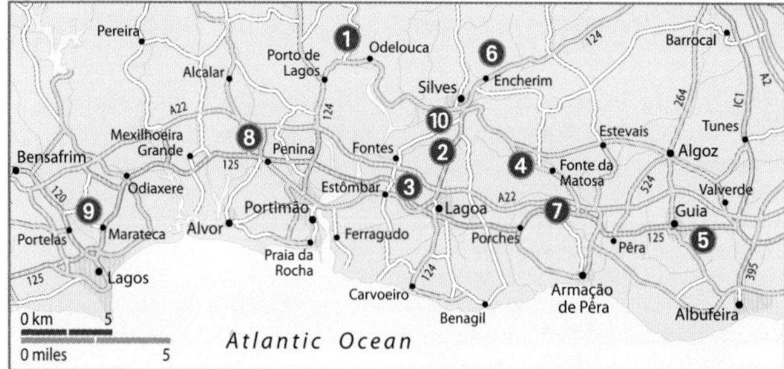

⑥ Quinta Rosa

MAP F4 ■ Pinheiro e Garrado, near Silves ■ (968) 986 393 ■ Closed Aug ■ Guided tours only: advance booking required ■ www.quinta-rosa.nl

This Dutch-run vineyard is behind the select Uit de Kelders Van Jaap wine label. Utilizing organic farming techniques, the estate produced its first harvest in 2011 and now offers tours, tastings and plenty of amusing anecdotes. Volunteers can help with grape picking in exchange for board and lodging.

⑦ Quinta João Clara

MAP F4 ■ Vale de Lousas, near Alcantarilha ■ (967) 012 444 ■ Open 11am–5pm Mon–Thu, 10am–5pm Fri–Sun ■ Advance booking required ■ www.joaoclara.com

No fewer than six wines are produced at this family-run vineyard, which occupies land farmed since the 1970s. Well respected in industry circles (the João Clara red is a multi-award winner), the various wines can be tasted as part of a tour of the premises. For added flavour, visitors can request an optional ham and cheese accompaniment.

⑧ Quinta da Penina

Part of a large family-run estate just north of Alvor *(see p50)* and owned by expert agronomist João Mariano, Quinta da Penina *(see p87)* is a stalwart of the Algarve's many established wineries. Tours of this grand estate are conducted for groups of ten or more. Tastings allow a variety of wines to be sampled, representing two separate labels. Mid-range choices include the Foral de Portimão Petit-Verdot red and, for a treat, the elegant and full-flavoured Quinta da Penina Reserva.

⑨ Monte da Casteleja

MAP D4 ■ Sargaçal, near Lagos ■ (912) 417 907 ■ Open 3–5pm Tue–Thu; Shop: 10am–1pm daily ■ Advance booking required ■ www.montecasteleja.com

The grapes used to produce the highly regarded reds, whites and rosés at this tranquil winery are grown organically here *(see p27)*. Rustic-style accommodation is also available.

Rustic Monte da Casteleja

⑩ Quinta de Mata Mouros

MAP F4 ■ Silves ■ Guided tours only: advance booking required ■ www.conventodoparaiso.com

Set in the hills beyond Silves, this relatively new winery has been cultivating a huge vineyard since 2000. The Euphoria red, white and rosé have gathered quite a following over the past two decades.

Top 10 Shopping Malls and Markets

1 Quinta Shopping, Quinta do Lago

This elegant mall *(see p87)* with its open-air terraces and wide esplanades is situated within the exclusive Quinta do Lago estate. Well-known fashion houses showcase their latest ready-to-wear designs, and there are some top-range jewellery, cosmetics and perfumes for sale. This is the place to go if you are looking to spend some serious cash.

Elegant Quinta shopping mall

2 Algarve Shopping, Guia

The exterior of this shopping complex *(see p87)* is striking in its colour scheme, following the geometric pattern of traditional Algarve architecture. Inside, the mall boasts more than 130 stores, 45 fashion boutiques, a hypermarket as well as a food hall.

3 Quarteira Fish Market

One of the best-loved fish markets *(see p87)* in the region, where the catch is landed at dawn and on sale by 8:30am. Be prepared to haggle on prices and to compete with others for the best fish. Note that the throng is usually largest around the famous Quarteira prawns.

4 Olhão Market

MAP L5 ■ Avenida 5 de Outubro, Olhão ■ Open 7am–2pm Tue–Fri, 6:30am–3pm Sat

Situated right on the esplanade overlooking the lagoons, this is a fantastic place to shop for fresh fish, fruit and vegetables and flowers. A riot of noise and colour takes place under two purpose-built pavilions. On Saturdays it is enlivened by extra stalls selling anything from basketware and smoked sausage, to honey and lace.

5 Forum Algarve, Faro

Forum Algarve is the biggest mall *(see p87)* of its kind in the whole region, attracting visitors and residents alike. More than 100 shops, boutiques and department stores, as well as an enormous hypermarket, multi-screen cinema and family entertainment centre, are imaginatively incorporated into an architectural design inspired by Faro's historic city centre.

The expansive Forum Algarve

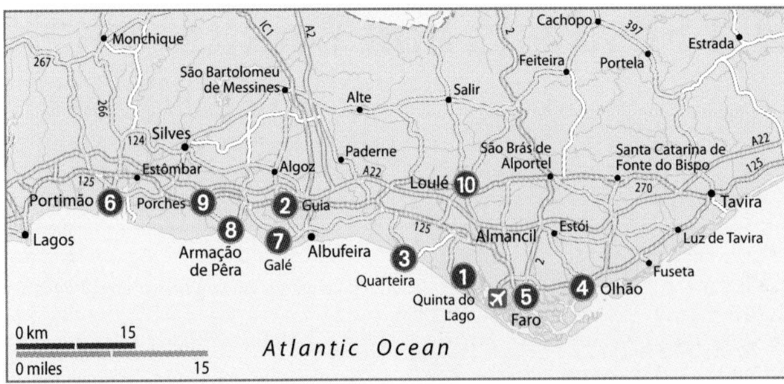

6 Aqua Portimão

MAP E4 ■ Rua de São Pedro 72, Portimão ■ Open 9am–11pm daily (to midnight Fri & Sat, Jul, Aug & Dec) ■ www.aqua-portimao.klepierre.pt

Centrally located, this shopping mall features nearly 80 shops, boutiques and a huge hypermarket. There are several ATMs, and underground car parking is free. The top floor is all restaurants.

7 Apolónia Supermarket, Galé

MAP J5 ■ Sítio Vale do Rebelho, Galé ■ Open 8am–8pm daily (summer: to 9pm)

Shoppers in the know travel here from across the length and breadth of the region. The market features foreign produce such as fresh Argentinian beef, macaroni pasta and spicy tandoori curry powder. The cosmopolitan wine selection includes bottles from California, Chile and Australia. There are two other branches, one in Almancil *(see p87)* and another in Lagoa.

8 Armação de Pêra Fruit and Fish Market

MAP F5 ■ Behind Largo da Igreja, Armação de Pêra ■ Open 7am–1pm Wed & Sat

This indoor and outdoor market has an amazing choice of fresh fruit and fish, including crab, lobster and clams. Outside you will find stalls selling jams, honey and tongue-tingling *piri-piri*.

Urn, Porches Pottery

9 Porches Pottery

The blue and white façade of this building *(see p87)* is unmistakable, and the pottery produced here is equally striking. All the pottery and earthenware on sale has been manufactured in-house, and you can see rows of locals gossiping merrily amongst themselves while deftly applying paint to the latest batch of crockery.

10 Loulé Market

This daily market *(see p87)* bursts with the freshest harvest from the ocean and the hinterland. Delicate sprigs of herbs and spices hang over pots of honey and jam. Cakes made from fig and almond compete for space with loops of smoked sausage, glistening fresh fish, and the numerous blooms of bright, fragrant flowers.

An array of produce at Loulé Market

TOP 10 Festivals and Events

Flower Torches Festival

1 Flower Torches Festival

MAP K4 ■ São Brás de Alportel town centre ■ Easter Sun

Dozens of suited men holding aloft elaborate bouquets of flower torches line a "flower pavement" – a series of roads decorated with carpets of colourful petals that a religious procession follows as it makes its way towards the parish church. Set near the church, a handicrafts fair opens mid-morning, and there's another fair selling local delicacies at Largo S. Sebastião.

2 Mãe Soberana, Loulé

MAP J4 ■ Loulé town centre ■ Usually last week in Apr

This is the Algarve's most important religious festival, linked to ancient maternity rites. On the second Sunday after Easter (Festa Grande), a 16th-century statue of Mãe Soberana (the Sovereign Mother) is carried into town from her hilltop shrine. Exuding solemnity and piety, the subdued procession makes its way to Loulé's parish church where the image rests for two weeks. On the return journey the mood is more ebullient – flowers are tossed at the cortège, and there are cries of "Viva Mãe Soberana!"

3 Festival Med, Loulé

MAP J4 ■ Loulé ■ Last week in Jun ■ www.festivalmed.pt

This festival celebrates the Algarve's Mediterranean and North African culture through concerts, culinary events, art exhibitions and children's activities, held in and around Loulé. It also includes world-class acts from Brazil, the Caribbean and sub-Saharan Africa. Many of the town's monuments – such as the castle and Islamic bathhouse *(see pp22–3)* – serve as festival venues.

4 Mercado de Culturas à Luz das Velas, Lagoa

MAP E4 ■ Lagoa ■ 4–7 Jul

Lit by more than 12,000 flickering candles, this atmospheric outdoor market illuminates the seaside town of Lagoa and celebrates the cultural diversity of the region. Over the course of four nights, more than sixty skilled craftspeople from a variety of cultures and religions display their traditions, gastronomy and arts. Not only is this event beautiful to look at, it's also a fantastic place to purchase locally made products, wine and international delicacies.

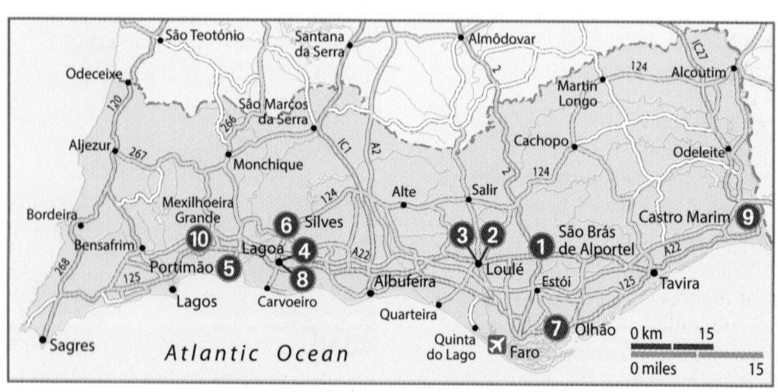

5 Portimão Sardine Festival

MAP E4 ■ Portimão riverfront ■ Usually 1st week in Aug

Generally regarded as the sardine capital of the Algarve, Portimão throws a big party in summer to honour this venerable fish. Revellers are drawn to the riverfront by live music and the delicious aroma of grilled sardines. On the last night, there is a huge firework display.

6 Silves Medieval Fair

MAP F4 ■ Silves ■ Second week in Aug ■ Adm for jousting displays

Silves returns to its former medieval splendour during this festival, when the centre's narrow streets and alleys become one huge souk. Visitors can enjoy parades, live music, street theatre and jousting competitions.

Silves Medieval Fair

7 Seafood Festival, Olhão

MAP L5 ■ Jardim Patrão Joaquim Lopes, Olhão ■ 10–15 Aug ■ www.festivaldomarisco.com

Olhão is the Algarve's biggest fishing port, and at festival time numerous stalls groan under the weight of every imaginable seafood delicacy, including octopus, squid, clams, prawns, mussels and the ubiquitous grilled sardine. Folk music and dancing add further flavour.

8 Fatacil, Lagoa

MAP E4 ■ Fatacil showground, EN 125, Lagoa ■ Mid-Aug ■ www.fatacil.pt ■ Adm

The premier showcase for all things Algarve, this nine-day jamboree attracts visitors from all over Portugal. It is part agricultural show, part handicrafts fair – with a music concert, trade exhibition and gastronomy festival thrown in for good measure.

9 Medieval Fair, Castro Marim

MAP P3 ■ Castro Marim ■ Last week in Aug ■ Adm

For a few days towards the end of the summer the town of Castro Marim returns to the Middle Ages to host a spectacular pageant and fair in the grounds of the 13th-century castle. Archers draw their bows on mock bullseye targets while mounted knights tilt their lances, and jesters entertain the crowd with medieval music and banter. At night, actors in period costume recreate medieval plays before a hushed audience.

10 Algarve Classic Car Festival

MAP D4 ■ Autódromo Internacional do Algarve, Mexilhoeira Grande ■ 3rd weekend in Oct ■ www.autodromodoalgarve.com ■ Adm

Hundreds of legendary sports cars can be seen at this remarkable annual event. Various races take place for different categories of vehicle. Previous events have attracted many celebrated drivers such as Walter Röhrl.

Algarve Classic Car Festival

The Algarve Area by Area

Sea caves at Ponta da Piedade, Lagos

TOP 10 Central Region

The Algarve's central region encompasses the busiest coastal resorts in southern Portugal as well as remote inland hamlets. It is an area of contrasting character, with beautiful golden beaches and wild, rolling hills where a more traditional, rural way of life prevails. History has left its indelible mark throughout this land in the shape of Stone Age megaliths, the remains of Roman villas, Moorish castles and Gothic cathedrals. A strong, proud maritime heritage pervades the coast, evident in the many fine seafood restaurants.

1 Silves

The capital of the Algarve during Moorish rule, Silves overlooks a fertile valley of lemon and orange groves, cork and almond trees and scented meadows. The town's main draw is its castle: as well as taking an inspiring walk around its battlements, visitors should look out for the vaulted Moorish cistern and traitor's gate – the battle-scarred doorway through which Dom Paio Peres Correia stormed to recapture the stronghold for Christian forces in 1242. Outside the castle walls is the 13th-century cathedral *(see pp18–19)*, which was the seat of the Algarve see until 1580.

2 Albufeira

Albufeira's claim as the most popular holiday destination in the country is no idle boast. It is

THE CENTRAL REGION

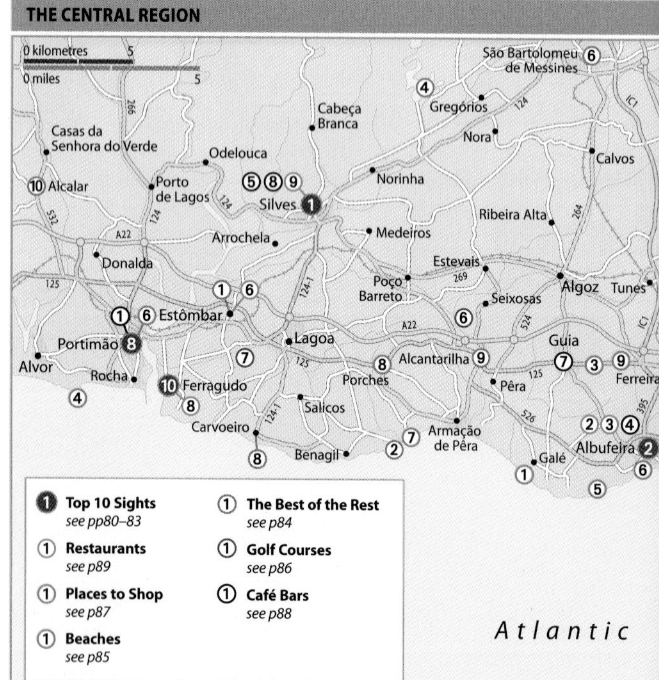

Top 10 Sights *see pp80–83*

The Best of the Rest *see p84*

Restaurants *see p89*

Golf Courses *see p86*

Places to Shop *see p87*

Café Bars *see p88*

Beaches *see p85*

Praia do Inatel, a popular beach in Albufeira

the biggest and most energetic resort *(see pp36–7)* in the Algarve, and anyone looking for a night out should make a midsummer beeline to the area dubbed "The Strip". A forest of neon lights and late-night entertainment, The Strip is known for its party atmosphere, numerous bars, restaurants and clubs. In the daytime, you can catch up on sleep on any one of Albufeira's smooth, golden beaches.

3 Faro

Faro is often overlooked by visitors to the Algarve who tend to head straight for the beach resorts. This is a shame because its Old Town *(see pp12–13)* quarter is a particularly enchanting ensemble of centuries-old architecture and fine museums. Among them is the former convent of Nossa Senhora da Assunção, which houses the excellent archaeological museum.

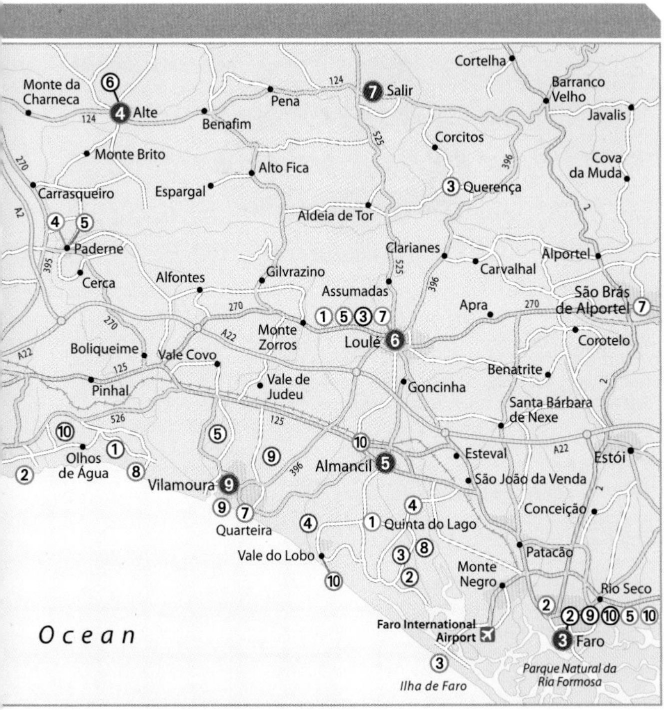

Monte da Charneca
Alte
Pena
Salir
Cortelha
Barranco Velho
Javalis
Benafim
Corcitos
Monte Brito
Alto Fica
Cova da Muda
Carrasqueiro
Espargal
Querença
Aldeia de Tor
Paderne
Clarianes
Alportel
Carvalhal
Cerca
Gilvrazino
Alfontes
Assumadas
São Brás de Alportel
Apra
Monte Zorros
Loulé
Corotelo
Boliqueime
Vale Covo
Benatrite
Pinhal
Vale de Judeu
Goncinha
Santa Bárbara de Nexe
Olhos de Água
Almancil
Esteval
Estói
Vilamoura
São João da Venda
Conceição
Quarteira
Quinta do Lago
Vale do Lobo
Patacão
Monte Negro
Rio Seco
Ocean
Faro International Airport
Faro
Ilha de Faro
Parque Natural da Ria Formosa

THE CAROB BEAN

The versatile carob bean tree is found throughout the Caldeirão mountain region. The beans are sometimes used as animal feed but also as a chocolate substitute. Pods can be ground and mixed with wheat flour to make tasty black bread. The gum is used in the textile and pharmaceutical industries.

Alte

MAP H3

Described as "a delightful snapshot of the real Algarve" in many a tourist brochure, Alte is indeed a picture of beauty and serenity. The little village with its whitewashed façades, cobbled streets, filigree chimney pots and rural charm appears to have little time for the 21st century, but always greets visitors with a warm smile. The central attraction is the picnic spot near the stream. The area is also renowned for its handicrafts and colourful folklore.

Almancil

MAP J5

One of the most resplendent of all the Algarve's treasures is the 18th-century Igreja Matriz de São Lourenço *(see p22)*, just outside Almancil. Outstanding *azulejo* panels in the church depict episodes in the life of St Lawrence, while the highly ornate cupola is a breathtaking exercise in trompe l'oeil – indeed, some say it is the best example of its kind outside Rome.

Almancil *azulejo*

6 Loulé

This cheerful market town *(see pp22–3)* is renowned as a centre of traditional handicrafts. The copper, leather and ceramic goods hammered out in the dozens of workshops dotted around its streets are some of the most sought after in the Algarve. These can be purchased at Loulé's market *(see p77)*, along with an amazing selection of fruit and vegetables, fresh fish, herbs, cheeses, spices, honey, bottled liqueurs and sugared fig cakes. Loulé was an important Moorish settlement, and remnants of Muslim rule still exist.

Salir

MAP J3

In springtime, wild flowers of every hue blanket the meadows around this hilltop hamlet, with its ruined 12th-century Moorish castle *(see p44)* and small museum. The terraced battlements are now reclaimed to ingenious effect by enterprising locals who use them as vegetable plots. The short walk around the castle foundations is rewarded with an inviting panorama over the limestone massif of Rocha da Pena. The area is a well-known nesting site for the huge eagle owl. Naturalists may also be lucky enough to spy a common genet or an Egyptian mongoose.

8 Portimão

Portimão's *(see pp38–9)* esplanade is lined with pretty gardens and a variety of restaurants and cafés. This is the departure point for sightseeing cruises along the Arade River; it is also the location of the excellent Museu de Portimão *(see p47)*. Nearby are the Autódromo Internacional do Algarve, a world-class racing track, and Ocean Revival Park, a unique artificial reef made of sunken warships, perfect for diving.

Castle of São João, near Ferragudo

9 Vilamoura

MAP H5

With its glamorous reputation, Vilamoura is the resort choice for yachters and minor celebrities. The boardwalk is also the jumping-off point for coastal cruises on graceful schooners. The region as a whole is of great environmental and historical significance – the wetland surrounding the resort is a protected nature reserve, and the Museu Cerro da Vila *(see p46)* is one of the most important Roman sites in Portugal.

Marina at Vilamoura

10 Ferragudo

MAP E5

Ferragudo has admirably managed to avoid the more garish trappings of tourism and looks better for it. Sitting at the mouth of the Rio Arade, this attractive fishing village tumbles down to a busy little quayside tightly packed with fishermen's huts, artisan's workshops and one or two truly memorable seafood restaurants *(see p89)*. The maze of steep alleys lead up to a handsome church. Praia Grande is a generous swathe of sand, which is popular sunbathing territory, and also the location of a big windsurfing school.

A TOUR OF VILLAGES

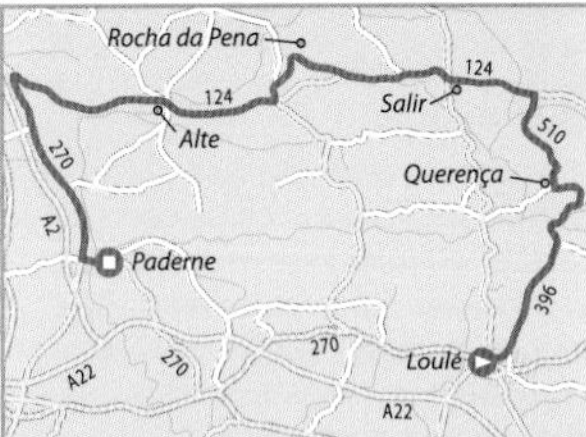

MORNING

An ideal starting point for your drive is **Loulé** where the highlight is most definitely its market. An early start will ensure you get the best choice of the produce. Aim to arrive at about 9am and allow an hour for browsing the stalls.

Order a coffee in Café Calcinha *(Praça da República 67)* before jumping in the car and heading north on the N396 to the quaint hamlet of **Querença** *(see p84)* with its whitewashed church and ancient stone cross. Take time to soak up the rural atmosphere, perhaps over a snack, at one of the cafés overlooking the square.

Head north for **Salir** on the M510, a meandering drive that weaves through woodland, before turning west on the N124. Explore the castle ruins and admire the superb views of the **Rocha da Pena** limestone plateau. If you have arrived on a weekday, the little archaeological museum next to the castle will be open.

AFTERNOON

Continue on the N124 to **Alte** for lunch, perhaps at one of the traditional cafés located near the church. Then allow an hour to explore one of the Algarve's prettiest villages and shop for traditional handicrafts.

End the afternoon by continuing to **Paderne** *(see p84)*, reached by travelling west on the N124 and then south on the N270. Follow the signs to visit the 12th-century Moorish castle *(see p44)*.

See map on pp80–81

The Best of the Rest

1 Estômbar

MAP E4

From this village follow the signs to Sítio das Fontes and discover a delightful hideaway picnic spot overlooking the Arade river. An old watermill can be seen among the beautiful surroundings.

Capela de Nossa Senhora da Rocha

2 Forte e Capela de Nossa Senhora da Rocha

MAP F5

Perched on a promontory, the tiny 15th-century chapel of Our Lady of the Rock is noted for its unusual octagonal cupola. The clifftop views take in eccentric rock formations and a beautiful golden beach.

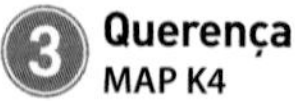

3 Querença

MAP K4

A charming, hill-top hamlet slumbering in isolated beauty and crowned by the simple Igreja Nossa Senhora da Assunção.

4 Barragem do Arade

MAP F3

Birdsong echoes around this huge, picturesque reservoir, which makes a wonderful picnic spot. The rolling countryside is great hiking and mountain-biking territory.

5 Paderne

MAP G4

A world away from the villas and beaches of the Algarve coast. Paderne's faded, timeworn charm is mirrored in the village by some lovely 19th-century buildings. Several friendly café-restaurants dotted around the vicinity provide welcome refreshment.

6 São Bartolomeu de Messines

MAP G3

Poet João de Deus (1830–96) is synonymous with this quiet rural town. The church has some amazing twisted sandstone pillars, which are unique in the Algarve.

7 Calçadinha Roman Road

MAP D4 ■ Interpretation Centre: Rua do Matadouro 2, São Brás de Alportel; (289) 840 004; 9:30am–1pm & 2–5:30pm Tue–Sat

The Calçadinha, or cobbled street, is 1,480 m (4,855 ft) in length. It was part of the region's Roman road network and can still be walked.

8 Praia do Carvoeiro

MAP E5

This picturesque beach is wedged between steep-sided cliffs and is framed by rows of holiday apartments and restaurants. It is a popular spot for families in the summer, and for golfers during the winter months.

9 Alcantarilha

MAP F4

This village is known for its bone chapel, where the skeletal remains of 1,500 former parishioners cover the ceilings and walls.

10 Alcalar

MAP D4

The Alcalar burial chambers *(see p38)* are a series of Megalithic tombs. The drive here is a delight in itself, passing through rows of ancient oak and olive trees.

Beaches

1 Praia da Galé, Armação de Pêra

MAP F5

Two half-moons of smooth white sand make up this beach, interrupted only by some unusual outcrops of ochre-splashed sandstone.

2 Praia da Oura, Albufeira

MAP G5

Located at the bottom of "The Strip", this is a hugely popular beach in summer, and attractive too, with its patches of yellow sandstone rock.

3 Praia de Faro, Ilha de Faro

MAP J6–K6

One of the narrow barrier islands that shelter the Ria Formosa lagoon, this giant sand spit is a magnet for Faro residents, and for those visitors wishing to escape the city heat.

4 Praia da Rocha, Portimão

MAP E4

One of the most famous beaches in the Algarve, this impressive swathe of golden sand stretches out in front of russet-coloured cliffs.

5 Praia de São Rafael, Albufeira

MAP G5

Some extraordinary rock formations protrude from the shallows of this pretty bay, fringed with fine sand.

Rock formations at Praia de São Rafael

Beachgoers at Praia dos Pescadores

6 Praia dos Pescadores, Albufeira

MAP G5

This beach is named for the colourful fishing boats that between use, were once left on the sand *(see p36)*. The vessels now moor up in the marina.

7 Praia da Senhora da Rocha

MAP F5

Warm, clear waters lap this inviting envelope of sand, framed between high cliffs. The beach is overlooked by the chapel, Forte e Capela de Nossa Senhora da Rocha.

8 Praia da Falésia, Olhos de Água

MAP H5

A long, narrow beach that never gets too crowded, even in summer. It is exposed to fresh southwesterly winds, which attracts the windsurfing set. A good option if you are in search of some peace and quiet.

9 Praia de Vilamoura

MAP H5

The beach at Vilamoura enjoys an enviable location right next to the resort. Its waters are calmed by the harbour breakwater, and the place is often used as a backdrop by fashion photographers.

10 Praia de Vale do Lobo

MAP J5

This select beachfront is patronized by guests staying at the nearby Vale do Lobo resort. There are some excellent bar-cafés close by.

See map on pp80–81

Golf Courses

Panoramic view of the Pine Cliffs golf course

1 Pine Cliffs

MAP G5 ■ Praia da Falésia, Albufeira ■ (289) 500 113

This 9-hole, par 33 clifftop course is set against a spectacular Atlantic Ocean backdrop. The last hole is named "Devil's Parlour" *(see p60)*.

2 San Lorenzo

MAP J5 ■ Quinta do Lago ■ (289) 396 522

This magnificent, 18-hole, par 72 course is considered by *World Golf* magazine to be one of Europe's top five golf courses *(see p60)*.

3 Quinta do Lago South

MAP J5 ■ Almancil ■ (289) 390 705

Quinta do Lago South, a famous championship course, has hosted the Portuguese Open several times. It is notable for four challenging par 5 holes *(see p61)*.

4 Vale do Lobo

MAP J5 ■ Almancil ■ (289) 353 465

The Royal Course incorporates the world-famous par 3 16th hole with an extensive carry over cliffs *(see p60)*. The Ocean Course follows an undulating layout.

5 Vilamoura Golf Courses

MAP H5 ■ Vilamoura ■ (289) 310 333

The Old Course, Pinhal, Laguna, Millennium and Victoria *(see p60)* are 18-hole, par 72 layouts, in beautifully landscaped settings.

6 Amendoeira Faldo & O'Connor Jnr

MAP F5 ■ Amendoeira Golf Resort, EN 529, Alcântarilha ■ (289) 310 333

The Amendoeira Golf Resort has two acclaimed 18-hole layouts – designed by golfers Sir Nick Faldo and Christy O'Connor Jnr.

7 Vale da Pinta Course, Pestana Carvoeiro

MAP E5 ■ Pestana Golf & Resort, Carvoeiro ■ (282) 340 900

An ancient olive tree spreads over one of the greens of the 18-hole Pinta course, while the 18-hole Gramacho layout has some heavily bunkered greens.

8 Pinheiros Altos

MAP J5 ■ Quinta do Lago ■ (289) 359 910

An independent 27-hole, par 72 course built on the Quinta do Lago estate, embracing part of the Parque Natural da Ria Formosa.

9 Vila Sol Golf

MAP H5 ■ Morgadinhos, Vilamoura ■ (289) 320 370

Known for its water hazards, this 27-hole, par 72 course is a challenge for golfers of all handicap levels.

10 Balaia Golf

MAP G5 ■ Albufeira ■ (289) 570 200

This executive 9-hole, par 27 course *(see p61)* is built on undulating terrain, punctuated with umbrella pine and cork oak trees.

Places to Shop

1 Loulé Market

MAP J4 ■ Praça da República, Loulé ■ Open 7am–3pm Mon–Sat

This market sells fruit and vegetables, fish, herbs, spices, cheeses, flowers and local handicrafts *(see p75)*.

2 Forum Algarve Shopping Centre

MAP K6 ■ EN 125, Sítio das Figuras, Faro ■ Open 10am–midnight daily

With an architectural design inspired by Faro's historical centre, this is the region's biggest shopping mall *(see p74)*.

3 Algarve Shopping Centre

MAP G4 ■ EN 125, Guia ■ Open 10am–midnight daily

A modern mall with national and international chains, a cinema and a food hall *(see p74)*.

4 Quinta Shopping Mall

MAP J5 ■ Quinta do Lago ■ Open 10am–7pm daily (to midnight Jul & Aug)

An elegant open-air mall with several designer boutiques, sports outlets and restaurants *(see p74)*.

5 Sardinha

MAP J4 ■ Largo D. Pedro I, 3, Loulé ■ (289) 512 936 ■ Open 10am–7pm Mon–Fri (to 3pm on Sat); Closed Sun

The humble sardine is just one source of inspiration for the many souvenirs sold at this quirky studio.

6 Quinta da Penina

MAP E4 ■ Rua da Angola Lote 2, Loja B+C, Portimão ■ (282) 491 070 ■ Guided tours only: advance booking required ■ www.vinhosportimao.com

Wine tastings and tours are held regularly at this excellent winery *(see p73)*. Visitors can also make the most of discounted prices at the Quinta da Penina shop.

7 Quarteira Fish Market

MAP H5 ■ Largo do Peixe, Quarteira ■ Open 8:30am–1:30pm Mon–Sat

The most famous market *(see p74)* of its kind on the south coast; arrive early for the best choice of fish and seafood.

Urn, Porches Pottery

8 Porches Pottery

MAP F4 ■ EN 125, Porches, Lagoa ■ Open 9am–6pm Mon–Fri, 10am–2pm Sat

One of the first commercial ceramic outlets *(see p75)* in the region.

9 Gigagarden

MAP G4 ■ Guia, EN 125 ■ Open 9am–7:30pm Mon–Sat, 10am–7pm Sun

This sprawling garden centre displays a variety of shrubs, trees and cacti.

10 Apolónia Supermarket

MAP J5 ■ Avenida 5 de Outubro, 271, Almancil ■ Open 8am–8pm daily (summer: to 9pm)

The best supermarket in the country for imported produce that is difficult to buy elsewhere in Portugal.

The bakery at Apolónia Supermarket

See map on pp80–81

Café Bars

1 Casa da Isabel, Portimão

MAP E4 ■ Rua Direita 61, Portimão ■ Closed Wed ■ www.acasadaisabel.com ■ €

This wonderful little teahouse is hidden behind the tiled façade of a Portimão townhouse. The cakes, teas and coffees are said to be the town's best.

2 Maktostas, Faro

MAP K6 ■ Rua do Alportel 29, Faro ■ (916) 300 517 ■ €

Set on a pretty square in a peaceful corner of the town, this characterful spot serves seafood, traditional meat dishes, vegetarian and vegan fare.

3 Café Calcinha, Loulé

MAP J4 ■ Praça da República 67, Loulé ■ (964) 066 842 ■ €

Enjoy a cup of strong Portuguese coffee at Calcinha. Serving caffeine shots since 1927, it's the town's oldest café.

4 Casa da Fonte, Albufeira

MAP G5 ■ Rua João de Deus 7, Albufeira ■ www.restaurantebarcasadafonte.pt ■ €€

With its urban decor, friendly service and great grilled fish and meat dishes, this is a must visit spot for lunch in Albufeira.

5 Pastelaria Rosa, Silves

MAP F4 ■ Largo do Município, Silves ■ Closed Sun ■ www.darosa.pt ■ €

A superb spot to try traditional Algarve pastries and great coffee.

6 Agua Mel, Alte

MAP H3 ■ Largo José Cavaco Veira, Alte ■ Closed Sun ■ €

A fine retreat after a day in the mountains, this café provides far-reaching views to accompany its coffees, snacks and light lunches.

7 Ramires, Guia

MAP G5 ■ Rua 25 de Abril, Guia ■ (289) 561 232 ■ No veg dishes ■ €

Diners have been flocking to this casual eatery since 1964 for what's said to be the best chicken piri-piri in the Algarve.

8 Café Inglês, Silves

MAP F4 ■ Rua do Castelo 11, Silves ■ (282) 442 585 ■ €

Located below the castle, this café offers snacks plus mains and acts as a venue for live music, including *fado.*

9 Pigs and Cows, Faro

MAP K6 ■ Rua Baptista Lopes 57, Faro ■ Closed Tue & Wed ■ www.pigsandcowsalgarve.com ■ €€

The multi-cuisine menu and seasonal fare at this café is prepared with locally sourced ingredients.

10 Mavala Osteria Italiana, Faro

MAP K6 ■ Largo da Madalena 10, Faro ■ Closed Mon & Sun ■ (963) 100 473 ■ €€

The gourmet pastas, meat dishes, seafood and desserts make this an ideal stop for a quick lunch or less hurried evening dinner.

Elegant setting at Pastelaria Rosa, Silves

Restaurants

PRICE CATEGORIES
For a three-course meal for one with half a bottle of wine (or equivalent meal), taxes and extra charges.

€ under €30 €€ €30–€50 €€€ over €50

1 Casa Velha, Quinta do Lago

MAP J5 ■ Quinta do Lago ■ (289) 394 983 ■ D only ■ Closed Sun ■ €€€

It's easy to see why this fabulous dining spot has gained a listing in the Michelin Guide. Expect top-notch French cuisine with a Mediterranean twist and prices to match.

2 Dom Carlos, Albufeira

MAP G5 ■ Rua Alves Correia 100, Albufeira ■ (961) 475 618 ■ Closed Mon & Tue ■ €€€

The tasty cuisine at this formal restaurant, one of Albufeira's finest places for a special dinner, will have you coming back for more. It also serves a fantastic British-style Sunday roast.

3 Vila Joya, Albufeira

MAP G5 ■ Praia da Galé, Estrada da Galé, Albufeira ■ (289) 591 795 ■ Closed Wed ■ www.vilajoya.com ■ €€€

Set on the Atlantic coast, Albufeira's top restaurant serves gourmet cuisine and has an impressive wine list.

4 Veneza, Paderne

MAP G4 ■ Estrada de Paderne 560a ■ (289) 367 129 ■ Closed 15–31 May & 15–31 Oct ■ No veg dishes ■ €

A rural eatery famed for its rustic menu and vast selection of wine.

5 Vila Adentro, Faro

MAP K6 ■ Praça Dom Afonso III 17, Faro ■ (933) 052 173 ■ €€

This old town favourite is decked out in ancient *azulejos*, creating the setting for a memorable dining experience. The menu features one of the best traditional *cataplanas* in town and delicious local desserts.

Spread at O Charneco, Estômbar

6 O Charneco, Estômbar

MAP E4 ■ Rua Joaquim Manuel Charneco 3 ■ (282) 431 113 ■ Closed Sun ■ No credit cards ■ €

Diners at this lively restaurant enjoy a daily selection of seven courses of delicious regional fare, accompanied by a bottle of the house wine.

7 Bocage, Loulé

MAP J4 ■ Rua Bocage 14, Loulé ■ (289) 412 416 ■ Closed Sun ■ €

This long-standing establishment serves authentic Portuguese dishes including expertly grilled fish and meat complemented by exclusive local wine.

8 Sueste, Ferragudo

MAP E5 ■ Rua da Ribeira 91, Ferragudo ■ (282) 461 592 ■ Closed Sun & Jan ■ No veg dishes ■ €

Known for its range of seafood dishes, Sueste has its best tables on the quayside. The interior is set in a traditional Algarvian fishing cottage.

9 O Barradas, Silves

MAP F4 ■ Venda Nova, Palmeirinha, Silves ■ (282) 443 308 ■ Closed Wed ■ €€

Succulent meat, fresh fish and great service ensure a memorable dinner.

10 Faz Gostos, Faro

MAP K6 ■ Rua do Castelo 13, Faro ■ (914) 133 668 ■ €€€

This trendy Faro restaurant serves innovative meat and fish dishes using many locally sourced ingredients.

See map on pp80–81 ←

TOP 10 Eastern Region

Azulejos **at Estói**

Long, narrow sandbank islands stretch along much of the coastline of the eastern Algarve (Sotavento). These natural barriers shelter a fragile lagoon ecosystem that is home to an astounding variety of flora and fauna. Tucked behind them are time-worn fishing villages and hamlets. Further east, beautiful Renaissance churches loom over picturesque towns and elegant cities, replete with Roman bridges, Moorish castles and the distinctive pyramid-shaped rooflines. The sparse interior is nature's preserve, underlined by a culture and heritage that has remained unchanged for centuries.

EASTERN REGION

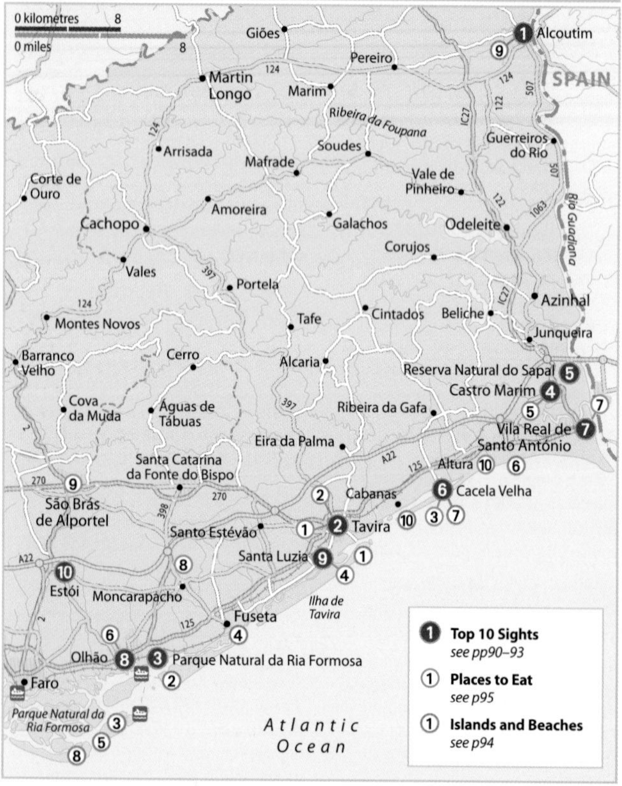

0 kilometres 8
0 miles 8

Alcoutim, Giões, Pereiro, Martin Longo, Marim, SPAIN, Ribeira da Foupana, Guerreiros do Rio, Arrisada, Soudes, Mafrade, Corte de Ouro, Vale de Pinheiro, Amoreira, Rio Guadiana, Cachopo, Galachos, Odeleite, Corujos, Vales, Portela, Azinhal, Montes Novos, Tafe, Cintados, Beliche, Junqueira, Barranco Velho, Cerro, Alcaria, Reserva Natural do Sapal, Castro Marim, Cova da Muda, Águas de Tábuas, Ribeira da Gafa, Vila Real de Santo António, Eira da Palma, Santa Catarina da Fonte do Bispo, Altura, Cacela Velha, Cabanas, São Brás de Alportel, Tavira, Santo Estêvão, Santa Luzia, Estói, Moncarapacho, Ilha de Tavira, Fuseta, Olhão, Parque Natural da Ria Formosa, Faro, Parque Natural da Ria Formosa, Atlantic Ocean

1 Top 10 Sights
see pp90–93

① Places to Eat
see p95

① Islands and Beaches
see p94

1 Alcoutim

MAP P1 ■ Castle: Apr–Sep: 9am–7pm daily (Oct–Mar: to 5pm) ■ Adm

The ramparts of a 14th-century castle *(see p44)* still stand vigil over this delightful riverside hamlet *(see p55)* that nestles on the upper reaches of the River Guadiana. On the Spanish side, the slumbering village of Sanlúcar de Guadiana amounts to a mirror image of Alcoutim. Once upon a time these two neighbours were at war with each other, and it was in the castle that a short-lived peace treaty was signed in 1371. A ferry now regularly shuttles between the two villages. Another way to cross the river is by zip line *(see p57)*.

2 Tavira

Churches are symbolic of Tavira *(see pp16–17)*, with nearly 40 towers and spires piercing the town's skyline. Two are of great historical significance: the Igreja da Misericórdia, the Algarve's most important Renaissance monument; and the Igreja de Santa Maria do Castelo, the final resting place of Dom Paio Peres Correia, who helped to retake Portugal from the Moors. The elegant Roman bridge spanning the River Gilão is another landmark that lends character to a town considered by many to be the most charming in the region.

The famous clockface of Igreja de Santa Maria do Castelo in Tavira

Parque Natural da Ria Formosa

3 Parque Natural da Ria Formosa

This vast realm of marshland, salinas and sand-dune islands is home to an incredible assortment of wildlife *(see pp30–33)*. The lagoon habitat is one of the most important wetland zones in Europe. The park's headquarters are near Olhão. Three exciting nature trails, São Lourenço, Quinta do Lago and Olhão, provide excellent opportunities for observing wildlife at close quarters.

4 Castro Marim

MAP P3

The time-worn frontier town of Castro Marim looms with genteel poise over the mouth of the River Guadiana, and its twin castles bear witness to the strategic importance that the settlement played during centuries past. Grand views from the ramparts of the main 13th-century stronghold *(see p45)* encompass the Reserva Natural do Sapal to the north and Vila Real de Santo António to the south. Spain shimmers in the distance.

5 Reserva Natural do Sapal

MAP P4

Much of this wetland park comprises working salt pans, but it is also a major winter feeding ground for spoonbill, greater flamingo, Kentish plover, avocet and other birds. The visitor centre (closed Sat and Sun) is on the edge of the salt marsh, and there is a lovely nature trail *(see p57)*.

The fortress at Cacela Velha

6 Cacela Velha

MAP N4

Thought to have been a Phoenician settlement in origin, this quaint coastal hamlet commands one of the most unspoiled locations in the Algarve. A patchwork of fields and meadows surround a bluff crowned by an 18th-century fortress. Lying in its shadow is the parish church; its whitewashed candescence plays off the façades of the fishermen's cottages lining the tiny square.

7 Vila Real de Santo António

MAP P4

The original settlement here was submerged by monstrous tidal surges in the early 17th century. It was reborn in the late 18th century, when the Marquês de Pombal designed a new town based on the Lisbon grid system. The town now attracts Spanish daytrippers from Ayamonte, just over the River Guadiana, which in turn is a magnet for sightseers from Portugal.

8 Olhão

MAP L5

One of the liveliest fishing ports in the Algarve, Olhão has some fine seafood restaurants. The whole town revolves around fishing, a fact exemplified by the 17th-century parish church, built with donations from the local fishermen. At the chapel of Nossa Senhora dos Aflitos, locals pray for the safe return of their loved ones during bad weather. The town's cube-shaped houses, with flat roof terraces and external staircases, reflect the close trade links once enjoyed with North Africa.

9 Santa Luzia

MAP M5

Stunted palmeiras, swaying lazily in the sea breezes, stud Santa Luzia's long esplanade. The village is synonymous with octopus, and dozens of empty *covos* (octopus pots) can be seen stacked near the quay, the hapless contents of which are probably on a dinner table. Summer sea safaris depart from the quayside and cruise the waters off Ilha de Tavira.

Fishing boats in Santa Luzia

CHARTLESS TO BRAZIL

In 1808, Olhão staged an uprising against the French garrison, which was the catalyst for Napoleon's retreat from Portuguese soil. In order to transmit the good news to King João VI in Brazil, a group of Olhão fishermen sailed to Rio de Janeiro, bereft of navigational charts. Their incredible voyage across the Atlantic so impressed the king that upon his return to the throne he elevated Olhão to town status.

Statue, Palácio do Visconde de Estói

10 Estói

MAP K5 ■ Milreu Roman Ruins: May–Sep: 9:30am–1pm & 2–6:30pm Tue–Sun; Oct–Apr: 9am–1pm & 2–5:30pm Tue–Sun; adm

The inland village of Estói basks in the glory of two major attractions: Palácio do Visconde de Estói *(see p54)* and the Roman ruins at nearby Milreu. The renovated 19th-century palace retains its pink Rococo façade and period architecture. Twenty minutes' walk away, the well-preserved Roman ruins include a peristyle villa built in the 2nd century AD, with baths decorated with fish mosaics and a temple.

A DRIVE TO ALCOUTIM

MORNING

A morning's drive north out of **Castro Marim** *(see p91)* on the EN122 will take you through undulating hills and lush valleys to the banks of the River Guadiana.

Allow a leisurely hour to reach **Alcoutim** *(see p91)*. Ignore the IC27 highway; stay on the EN122 towards Junqueira and Azinhal. After 30 minutes you will see a sign for Alcoutim on the right. Ignore this. Instead, carry on past the Barragem de Odeleite reservoir and several small hamlets. You will reach a junction at Cruzamento. Turn right here towards Alcoutim.

Pause for a coffee at any one of the cafés in Praça da República before exploring the castle *(see p44)* and its museum. Afterwards, have lunch back in the square.

AFTERNOON

If it is a hot day, saunter over to **Praia Fluvial de Alcoutim** *(see p94)*. Alternatively, catch the boat to neighbouring Spain and wander around Sanlúcar de Guadiana. Thrill seekers might want to return via the zip line *(see p59)*.

To return to Castro Marim, follow the EN507 south out of Alcoutim along the banks of the Guadiana for one of the most inspiring drives in the Algarve. Stop by the ruins of the Villa Romana do Montinho das Laranjeiras, a 1st century AD Roman dwelling.

After Foz de Odeleite, the road returns to the hills before joining the EN122 and heading south.

Islands and Beaches

1 Ilha de Tavira
MAP M5

A huge offshore sandbank stretching 11 km (7 miles) west from Tavira, connected to land by a 10-minute ferry from Quatro Águas. Alternatively, a mini railway can take you there from the resort of Pedras d'el Rei.

2 Ilha da Armona
MAP L5–6

Popular with independent travellers, the beaches facing inland are served by bars and restaurants. A ferry from Olhão takes 15 minutes.

3 Ilha da Culatra
MAP L6

The beaches here enjoy splendid isolation, and nude sunbathing in the dunes is not uncommon. The ferry takes 45 minutes from Olhão.

4 Ilha da Fuseta
MAP M5

You can walk onto this island at low tide. The beaches are exquisite, and the waters of the lagoon provide a popular destination for windsurfers.

5 Praia do Farol
MAP L6

A beautiful sweep of sand on the bank of a long island. Farol can be reached by taking a 45-minute ferry ride from the Porta Nova wharf below Faro's Old Town district. There are also regular departures from Olhão.

Tranquil Praia do Farol

6 Praia Verde
MAP P4

One of several beaches that follow the yawning curve of Monte Gordo Bay, the "green beach" is named after a verdant umbrella pine forest that fringes the sand.

7 Praia de Cacela Velha
MAP N4

Overlooked by the tiny Fortaleza Cacela Velha *(see p45)*, this secluded lagoon-fringed stretch of sand is perfect for sunbathing.

8 Ilha da Barreta
MAP K6

Boat departures from Faro's Porta Nova wharf shuttle visitors to this "deserted island", where wildlife can be observed. A bar-restaurant, O Estaminé, provides sustenance.

9 Praia Fluvial de Alcoutim
MAP P1

Known locally as Pego Fundo, this slither of sand fringing a tributary of the Guadiana is the only river beach in the Algarve.

10 Praia da Ilha de Cabanas
MAP N4

Less crowded than some of its neighbours, Cabanas' pristine beaches *(see p49)* lie in peaceful seclusion, and are reached by continuing westwards along the shores of Praia de Manta Rota.

Places to Eat

PRICE CATEGORIES

For a three-course meal for one with half a bottle of wine (or equivalent meal), taxes and extra charges.

€ under €30 €€ €30–€50 €€€ over €50

1 Brisa do Rio, Tavira

MAP M5 ■ Rua João Vaz Côrte Real 38 ■ (915) 434 452 ■ D only ■ Closed Wed & Nov ■ €

A regional dining hot spot, book in advance to secure a table at this acclaimed eatery.

2 A Ver Tavira, Tavira

MAP M4 ■ Calçada de Galeria, Tavira ■ (281) 381 363 ■ €€

A trendy eatery next to the castle with tapas and a *menú de dégustación*. Booking is essential.

3 Casa Velha, Cacela Velha

MAP N4 ■ Cacela Velha ■ (281) 952 297 ■ Closed Mon & Jan ■ No veg dishes ■ €

Set in a pretty hamlet, this quaint restaurant attracts an enthusiastic clientele for its *feijoada de longueirão* (razor clams in bean stew), oysters and other seafood dishes.

4 Marisqueira O Capelo, Santa Luzia

MAP M5 ■ Avenida Eng. Duarte Pacheco 40, Santa Luzia ■ (281) 381 670 ■ Closed Tue D, Wed & Jan ■ No veg dishes ■ €€

At a table on the terrace is the best way to savour this classic fish and seafood restaurant. Specialities include tuna stew and octopus rice.

5 A Tasca Medieval, Castro Marim

MAP P3 ■ Rua 25 de Abril 65 ■ (281) 513 196 ■ Closed Tue ■ No veg dishes ■ €

Top-notch food is served at this traditional restaurant. The house speciality *açorda de galinha* (bread-based chicken stew) must be ordered in advance, but it is worth the wait.

6 Restaurante Ria Formosa, Olhão

MAP L5 ■ Avenida 5 de Outubro 14 ■ (289) 702 504 ■ Closed Thu ■ No veg dishes ■ €

One local describes this much-loved restaurant as "an ocean under one roof". The menu bursts with catches, such as fresh *besugos* (mullet).

7 Os Arcos, Vila Real

MAP P4 ■ Avenida da República 45, Vila Real de Santo António ■ (281) 543 764 ■ €

A large, cavernous seafood restaurant on the town's riverfront.

Stylish interior at À Terra

8 À Terra, Moncarapacho

MAP L5 ■ Vila Monte Farm House, Sítio dos Caliços, Moncarapacho ■ (289) 790 790 ■ €€

Locally-sourced produce and herbs from the garden are used to prepare delicious meals, with a distinctly Mediterranean flavour.

9 Luís dos Frangos, São Brás de Alportel

MAP K4 ■ Rua Dr José Dias Sanchos 134, São Brás de Alportel ■ (289) 842 635 ■ Closed Mon and last 2 weeks Sep ■ No veg dishes ■ €

A down-to-earth eatery that serves up grilled chicken to tourists and locals.

10 A Chaminé, Altura

MAP N4 ■ Avenida 24 de Junho, Altura ■ (281) 950 100 ■ Closed Tue except Jul–Aug & 3rd week of Nov ■ €€

Noted by Michelin, particularly for its fish and seafood menu, this traditional restaurant is pleasant and homely.

See map on p90

TOP 10 Western Region

The Western Algarve (Barlavento) blends a precipitous Atlantic coastline with a green Mediterranean interior. The wild, windblown promontories associated with the legend of Henry the Navigator yield to forest-clad hills and cloud-tipped mountains. Some of the region's most spectacular beaches nestle on the south coast under outcrops of ochre-splashed rock. Underpinning all this is a rich historical thread of Baroque churches and Manueline chapels, stark sea defences and baffling Neolithic monuments. Visitor attractions abound, with quaint restaurants in hushed villages waiting to be discovered, and lively resorts with an international clientele.

Windmill, Odeceixe

WESTERN REGION

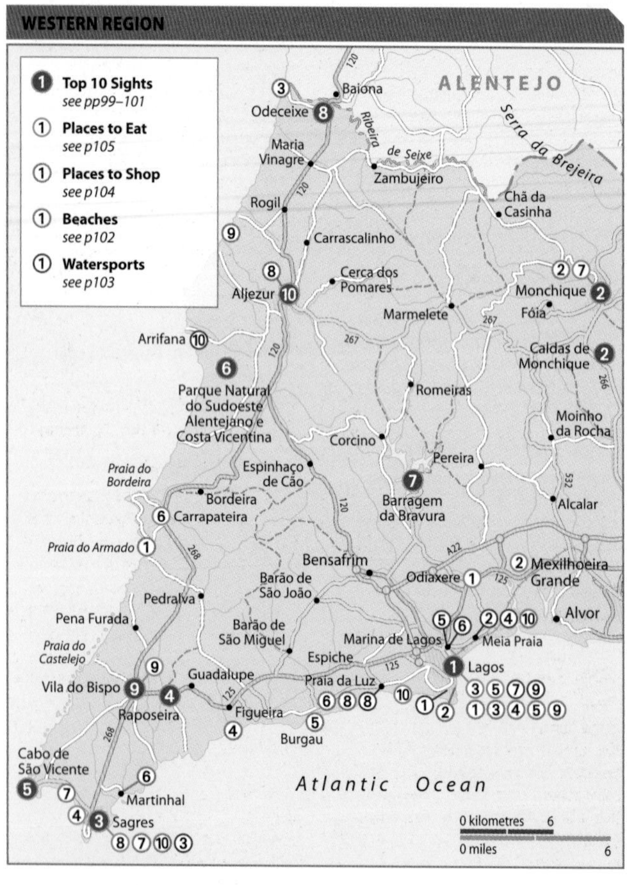

Previous pages *Praia do Camillo, Lagos*

The natural sea caves at Ponta da Piedade near Lagos

1 Lagos

One of the most popular resort towns in southern Portugal, Lagos *(see pp26–9)* immediately captures the imagination with its carefree holiday spirit, laid-back lifestyle and immense historical wealth. Its greatest treasure is the Igreja de Santo António. The nearby beaches are equally attractive, with their fine golden sand, ochre-splashed cliffs and bizarre outcrops of sandstone pillars.

2 Monchique and Caldas de Monchique

Monchique *(see pp20–21)*, a rustic little market town, is tucked away in the forested Serra de Monchique under a mantle of towering eucalyptus and magnolia. Nestling in its shadow is Caldas de Monchique, a charming leafy hamlet glowing in the fame of its renowned spa facility, where the sparkling mineral water is endowed with some remarkable curative properties. The Serra's unique Mediterranean-Atlantic habitat is a haven for wildlife. Sweeping views from Fóia and Picota crown this hugely diverse and fertile area.

3 Sagres

Sagres' claim to fame is the huge landmark fort spread across the arm of the precipitous Ponta de Sagres. It is here that Henry the Navigator's original fortress and the Vila do Infante – his legendary school of navigation – is said to have been located. Little remains of either except for perhaps the giant pebble Rosa dos Ventos (wind compass) and the plain little chapel of Nossa Senhora da Graça, both supposedly used by Henry in the 15th century. Sagres *(see pp34–5)* itself is a modest town bestowed with a pretty harbour and some magnificent beaches that attract surfers from around the globe.

Nossa Senhora da Graça in Sagres

4 Raposeira

MAP B5 ■ EN 125, Raposeira ■ Chapel: Open May–Sep: 10:30am–1pm & 2–6:30pm, Oct–Apr: 9am–1pm & 2–5:30pm; closed Mon; adm

The main attraction, located 1 km (half a mile) east of this small village, is the 14th-century chapel Nossa Senhora de Guadalupe, thought to be one of the oldest examples of Gothic architecture in the Algarve. Henry the Navigator was said to have prayed here when he lived in Raposeira, as did many a crew before departing for unknown lands. Inside the chapel, built in honour of the Virgin of Guadalupe, enigmatic stone heads peer down from the ceiling.

The cliffs of Cabo de São Vicente

5 Cabo de São Vicente

MAP B5

An austere landscape, dramatic limestone cliffs and a restless, unforgiving sea led Greek chroniclers to describe this windblown cape as the end of the earth. The Romans revered the rocky outcrop and called it Promontorium Sacrum, a place where the setting sun hissed in its dying embers as the ocean swallowed it up. The promontory retains an air of mystique. Henry the Navigator is said to have had a house in the small castle to the right of the lighthouse.

6 Parque Natural do Sudoeste Alentejano e Costa Vicentina

MAP B3–5 & C3 ■ Park headquarters: Rua Serpa Pinto 32, Odemira, Alentejo; (283) 322 735

The entire coastline of the western Algarve lies within the boundaries of this wild and rocky nature reserve. Dozens of scarce and endemic plant species thrive here – it is a botanist's paradise. Hundreds of different species of birdlife *(see p59)* flutter and glide above the coastal plains, while, not surprisingly, ornithologists gather with binoculars primed.

7 Barragem da Bravura

MAP D4

The huge, man-made lake 10 km (6 miles) north of Lagos is a wonderful place at which to unpack the picnic hamper. In spring, fields of orchids nestle under delicate umbrellas of almond blossom, with butterflies flitting from bloom to bloom. Towering eucalyptus encroach upon the lake-side, and the woods are a favourite haunt of red foxes and wild boar. The higher ground north of the dam is generously wooded with cork oak, and it is from this area that the best views of the lake can be enjoyed.

8 Odeceixe

MAP C1 ■ Windmill: Open Jun–Sep: 9am–noon & 2–6pm Tue–Sat

The River Seixe meanders past this pretty little village, which makes a handy base for surfers who are keen to ride the big swells that thunder onto Odeceixe beach. A lone windmill sitting above the village used to take advantage of the fresh winds whipped up by the Atlantic in days gone by. Today it is a popular vantage point for scanning the Alentejo countryside. This sleepy backwater is about as far

Parque Natural do Sudoeste Alentejano e Costa Vicentina

as you can get from the summer throngs that pack the coastal resorts. The good-value guesthouses found here fill up fast during the summer.

9 Vila do Bispo

MAP B4 ■ Menhir Circuit, Hortas do Tabual, Vila do Bispo

The landscape around Vila do Bispo is rich with evidence of the Algarve's prehistoric past *(see p57)*. Mysterious menhirs, also known as megaliths, dot the countryside. Near Hortas do Tabual, a number of these stones, some bearing crudely carved crosses, appear to form a circle. Archaeologists speculate that this could be the site of the mythical Church of the Raven, supposedly where the remains of St Vincent were interred before being taken to Lisbon.

Aerial view of Aljezur town

10 Aljezur

MAP C3

The humble ruins of a 10th-century Moorish castle *(see p44)* stand sentinel-like over a higgledy-piggledy collection of whitewashed houses and café-restaurants that constitute the village of Aljezur. A steep, cobbled path leads up to the time-worn but sturdy castle walls and the splendid view beyond. This riverine area was once a breeding ground for malaria-carrying mosquitoes, and in the 18th century some of the villagers were persuaded to relocate to Igreja Nova, Aljezur's "modern" counterpart to the east.

A TOUR OF THE WEST

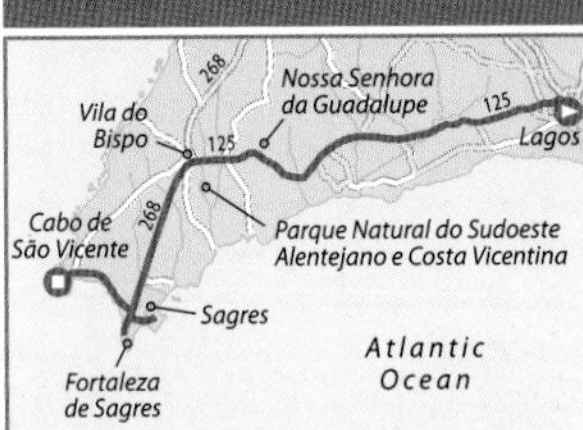

MORNING

Breakfast in **Lagos** *(see p99)* at the café in Praça Infante Dom Henrique near the castle walls, and then set out to explore the west coast.

The drive follows the EN125, crossing the boundary of the **Parque Natural do Sudoeste Alentejano e Costa Vicentina**. The road winds on – via the tiny 14th-century chapel of Nossa Senhora da Guadalupe and the prehistoric sights of **Vila do Bispo** – to **Sagres** *(see p99)* and its landmark 17th-century fort.

For an invigorating walk and to further appreciate the seascape at Sagres, follow the path around the promontory.

By now, it should be time for refreshments at Café-Restaurante Cochina on Praça da República. For something more substantial, try the Café-Restaurant Pau de Pita on Rua Comandante Matoso.

AFTERNOON

Sagres *(see p99)* has a pretty harbour, which can be investigated on foot. The nearby **Fortaleza de Sagres** *(see p45)*, the supposed location of Henry the Navigator's famed academy, is definitely worthy of an hour-long exploration.

No trip to the west coast would be complete without a visit to **Cabo de São Vicente**, which is a short drive northwest. The clifftop vistas are truly awe-inspiring and offer a suitably dramatic way to end the day.

See map on p98

Beaches

1 Praia do Amado, Carrapateira

MAP B4

One of the surfer's favourites *(see p48)*, Amado's Atlantic swells attract enthusiasts keen to ride the surf back into the wide sweeping beach.

Praia do Camilo, Lagos

2 Praia do Camilo, Lagos

MAP D5

A magical beach *(see p27)* and one of the most picturesque in the Algarve, Camilo *(see p48)* is framed by a collection of sandstone outcrops and a warren of caves and grottoes.

3 Praia de Odeceixe

MAP C1

The River Seixe runs into this delightfully secluded stretch of sand *(see p48)*, tucked away right up in the northern reaches of the Algarve.

4 Praia da Figueira, Figueira

MAP C5

Surrounded by tawny-hued cliffs, this beach is accessible only by foot, and can be reached by a narrow trail that meanders through a pretty valley.

5 Praia do Burgau

MAP C5

One of the best locations in the area for snorkelling and diving, the beach skirts Burgau resort and is hemmed in on either side by sloping cliffs.

6 Praia do Martinhal

MAP B6

A fabulous location for windsurfing, with the ocean lapping a golden swathe of sand. The beach is also conveniently situated near the town of Sagres.

7 Praia do Beliche, near Sagres

MAP B5

The steep climb down a cliff path to the beach is rewarded with a wonderfully secluded wedge of pristine sand. Due to its slightly awkward location, it does not tend to attract many visitors.

8 Praia da Luz

MAP C5

A fine beach, with very easy access to resort amenities, Praia da Luz can become crowded in high season. However, there is always some room, especially towards its eastern flank.

9 Praia de Monte Clérigo, Aljezur

MAP C2

Another beach preferred by keen surfers, and tourists that have a more independent spirit. This is a wild, isolated landscape with untamed breakers.

10 Meia Praia, Lagos

MAP D5

At 4 km (2 miles), this is one of the longest beaches *(see p49)* in the Algarve, allowing plenty of room for sunbathers to share the vista with water-skiers and windsurfers.

→ *See map on p98*

Watersports

1 Diving

MAP D5 ■ www.blue-ocean-divers.de

Explore caves, canyons, reefs and wrecks. Many schools also offer night dives, snorkelling safaris and PADI certification courses up to professional level.

2 Windsurfing

MAP D5 ■ www.algarvewatersport.com

The reliable winds off Meia Praia allow windsurfers to hone their skills in an expanse of open water perfectly suited to this popular sport.

3 Coasteering

MAP B6 ■ www.coastlinealgarve.com

Cliff-climbing, swimming in caves and ambling along coastal paths – this is coasteering, an exhilarating way in which to explore the area between Lagos and Sagres.

4 Kite Surfing

MAP E5–L6 ■ www.extremealgarve.com

One minute you are surfing, the next you are airborne. The best season for this watersport is May–Oct, and the flatwater lagoons near Lagos and Alvor are ideal locations.

5 Sailing

MAP D5 ■ www.southwesttrainingcenter.com

Sailing is ubiquitous in the Algarve, and there are plenty of schools in the region providing tuition. Cruise companies also charter yachts and organize sailing holidays.

6 Big Game Fishing

MAP D5 ■ www.pescamar.info

Several sports fishing operators are based in Marina de Lagos *(see p27)*, and use boats with state-of-the-art tackle and a fighting chair to pursue shark and marlin.

7 Paddleboarding

MAP D5 ■ www.jahshakasurf.com

Standup paddleboarding is one of the more novel methods of exploring the coastline. Options include night-time tours using innovative underwater lighting systems.

8 Water-skiing

MAP C5 ■ www.beachhutwatersports.com

Well sheltered from the wind, the waters off Praia da Luz provide an ideal arena in which to learn basic manoeuvres, practise wake crossings and try deep-water starts.

9 Kayaking

MAP D5 ■ www.kayak-lagos.com

Kayaking is a great way to see the grottoes and beaches around Lagos' beautiful Ponta da Piedade *(see p26)*.

10 Surfing

MAP B3 ■ www.arrifanasurfschool.com

West coast beaches such as Praia de Monte Clérigo and Praia do Castelejo are synonymous with surfing *(see p57)*. There are also a wide range of surf camps and schools around.

Surfing at Praia da Arrifana

Places to Shop

Shoppers on Rua Cândido dos Reis

1 Rua Cândido dos Reis/ Rua 25 de Abril, Lagos

MAP D5

The two busiest streets in town, where shoppers can browse the rows of stores and boutiques for jewellery, handicrafts and fashion.

2 Casa dos Arcos

MAP E3 ■ José Salvador, Estrada Velha, Monchique

One of the few places in the Algarve where you can purchase *cadeiras de tesoura*, the traditional folding wooden chairs, which are hand-crafted to an ancient Roman design.

3 Mediconforto

MAP D5 ■ Rua Soeiro da Costa 26, Lagos

A handy health-food shop selling a huge selection of minerals, vitamins, homeopathic remedies and natural cosmetics.

4 Atelier Opalina

MAP D5 ■ Praça do Infante 1, Lagos

A wide range of handmade jewellery fashioned out of gold, silver, mother-of-pearl, amber and precious stones.

5 Lagos Surf Center

MAP D5 ■ Rua Silva Lopes 31, Lagos ■ www.lagossurfcenter.com

An outlet for O'Neill, Rip Curl, Billabong and Quiksilver, you will find everything you need to surf here, including a choice of boards and beachwear. Staff can arrange rentals, surf schools and safaris, as well as accommodation.

6 Baptista Supermarket

MAP C5 ■ Montes da Luz, Praia da Luz ■ www.supermercado-baptista. com

Baptista is known for its fresh regional produce. On Saturdays there are occasional live cooking demonstrations, with tasting sessions later.

7 Sagres Natura Surf Shop

MAP B6 ■ Rua de São Vicente, Sagres

Come here for the wide range of top-brand surfwear, boards and accessories. The company also runs a well-established surf school, and rents kayaks and mountain bikes.

8 Aljezur Gypsy Market

MAP C3

A lively gypsy troupe trundles into Aljezur on the first Sunday of every month with an extraordinary array of clothing, household items and foodstuffs at bargain prices.

9 Mercado da Avenida

MAP D5 ■ Avenida dos Descobrimentos, Lagos ■ Open 8am–2pm Mon–Sat

A bustling fish market with a rooftop terrace restaurant and splendid views across the harbour.

10 Intermarché

MAP B6 ■ ER268, Sagres

On the main approach road to Sagres, this is the place at which to stock up on food, drink, toiletries and everyday essentials. Clothes, shoes, tools and kitchenware are also for sale. There is also an on-site café.

Places to Eat

PRICE CATEGORIES

For a three-course meal for one with half a bottle of wine (or equivalent meal), taxes and extra charges.

€ under €30 €€ €30–€50 €€€ over €50

1 Cacto, Odiáxere

MAP D4 ■ EN 125, Odiáxere ■ (282) 798 285 ■ Closed Wed & Thu ■ D only ■ €€

Creamy pepper, garlic or blue-cheese sauce tops the tournedos "fillet" steak at this lively eatery.

Shaded terrace at Cacto, Odiáxere

2 Adega Vila Lisa, Mexilhoeira Grande

MAP D4 ■ 52 Rua Francisco Bivar, Mexilhoeira Grande ■ (282) 968 478 ■ D only ■ Closed Oct–Jun: Sun–Thu No credit cards ■ No veg dishes ■ €€

A rural gem *(see p70)* with fine traditional cuisine, including succulent pork knee roast.

3 Mullen's, Lagos

MAP D5 ■ Rua Cândido Reis, 86, Lagos ■ (918) 480 071 ■ D only ■ Closed mid-Jan–Feb ■ €

This place is full of character and run by friendly staff. The Mozambique-style beef is incredible. Vegetarian food can be requested in advance.

4 O Terraço, Martinhal

MAP B6 ■ Hotel Martinhal, Martinhal ■ (282) 240 200 ■ D only ■ No veg dishes ■ €€€

A family-friendly restaurant, O Terraço *(see p70)* serves fresh regional food.

5 No Pátio, Lagos

MAP D5 ■ Rua Lançarote de Freitas 46, Lagos ■ (282) 763 777 ■ Closed Sun, Mon & last wk in Nov ■ €€

A charming alfresco restaurant that is popular with foodies.

6 Cabrita, Carrapateira

MAP B4 ■ 8670-230 Bordeira Carrapateira ■ (282) 973 128 ■ Closed Wed & Dec ■ No veg dishes ■ €

Located close to Praia do Amado *(see p102)*, this eatery serves fresh fish and seafood in a friendly atmosphere.

7 Bica Boa, Monchique

MAP E3 ■ Estrada de Lisboa, 266, Monchique ■ (282) 912 271 ■ €

Sit on the terrace during fine weather for a wholesome alfresco treat.

8 Vila Velha, Sagres

MAP B6 ■ Rua Patrão António Faustino, Sagres ■ (282) 624 788 ■ Tue–Sun D ■ Closed Jan & Feb ■ €€

Oven-baked stuffed quail with Muscatel wine and raisin sauce is just one of the eclectic dishes here.

9 A Eira do Mel, Vila do Bispo

MAP B5 ■ Estrada do Castelejo, Vila do Bispo ■ (282) 639 016 ■ Closed Sun & Mon L ■ €€

This rural Slow Food member offers a superb Atlantic wild-shrimp *cataplana* and delicious desserts.

10 Mirandus, Lagos

MAP D5 ■ Romantik Hotel Vivenda Miranda, Porto de Mós, Lagos ■ (282) 763 222 ■ Closed Nov–Mar ■ €€

This gourmet restaurant serves fantastic food and offers breathtaking views of the ocean and the coastline.

See map on p98 ←

TOP 10 The Alentejo

Undulating plains and blistering summer heat characterize much of this province to the north of the Algarve. Neatly combed vineyards embroider their way along huge tracts of land, and much of the sun-baked earth is pocked by stubby cork and olive trees. Whitewashed villages are surrounded by emerald vines growing on ochre soil. To the north, medieval settlements perch on steep, granite escarpments in an altogether rockier terrain. Down by the coast, secluded beaches of golden sand brush sleepy, unhurried resorts that wake up in summer, when the days are long and the air is warm.

Remains of the Templo Romano in Évora

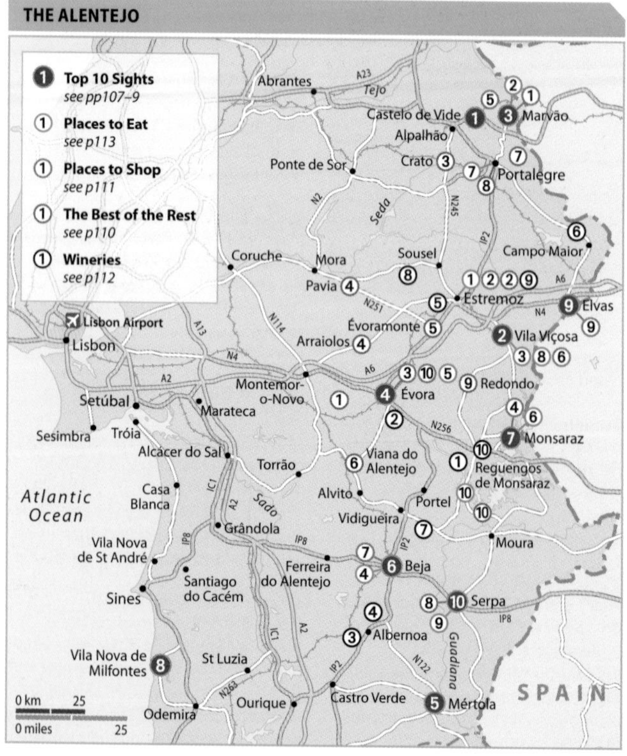

1 Castelo de Vide

Tourist info: Praça Dom Pedro V; (245) 901 361

The old Jewish quarter is the most enjoyable part of this attractive hilltop town. It stretches away from the 13th-century castle that gives the town its name in a cluster of steep lanes, many sporting plaques testifying to the quality of their floral displays. A synagogue (also 13th century) sits at the top of this stepped thoroughfare, which also leads down to the 16th-century marble Fonte da Vila.

2 Vila Viçosa

Tourist info: Praça da República; (268) 889 317

During the 15th century, Vila Viçosa became the country seat of the dukes of Bragança, and the town is best-known today for its splendid Paço Ducal. The sturdy battlements of the dukes' former abode, the castle, surround colourful cottages, two excellent museums and the 14th-century church of Nossa Senhora da Conceição.

3 Marvão

Tourist info: Rua da Silveirinha; (245) 909 131

Named "the eagle's nest" by locals, this medieval hamlet, set high upon on a rugged escarpment, is an astonishing sight. Sinuous 13th-century battlements envelop an immaculate village, where polished cobbled streets snake past neat façades, whitewashed cottages, a dainty church, trim gardens and a cherished museum. The castle has commanding views of the Serra de Marvão and the borderlands.

Fountain in Évora's Praça do Giraldo

4 Évora

Tourist info: Praça do Giraldo 73; www.visitevora.net

The historic centre of the capital of the Alentejo is listed as a UNESCO World Heritage Site. Stunning examples of Roman, Moorish, medieval and 17th-century architecture abound in the old town *(see p109)*. The central Praça do Giraldo has a wonderful 16th-century fountain. A walk from the square up the lively Rua 5 de Outubro leads to the grandiose Sé (cathedral). An adjacent 16th-century palace houses the Museu de Évora. Adega Cartuxa offers visitors a classic Portuguese wine *(see p112)*.

Stunning views of the Castelo de Marvão

The historic town of Mértola

5 Mértola

Tourist info: Rua da Igreja 31; www.visitmertola.pt

Designated a *vila museu*, or open-air museum town, the old quarter of Mértola is divided into a number of areas of historic interest. Each reflects diverse periods in the town's history: Phoenicians, Romans, Visigoths and Moors all took advantage of its strategic position on the River Guadiana. A number of museums exhibit treasures from each period, but the most stunning collection can be found in the Museu Islâmico.

6 Beja

Tourist info: inside the castle, Largo Dr Lima Faleiro; (284) 311 913

A thriving agricultural town and capital of the Baixo Alentejo, Beja also has a rich past displayed in museum buildings that are often as interesting as their exhibits. The Convento de Nossa Senhora da Conceição, for example, now houses the Museu Regional, and the town's oldest church – the 6th-century Santo Amaro – is home to the Museu Visigótico. The landmark Torre de Menagem (castle keep) dates from the late 13th century.

Nossa Senhora da Conceição in Beja

7 Monsaraz

Tourist info: Rua Direita; (927) 997 316

Swathes of vineyards surround Monsaraz, a name synonymous with some of the finest Portuguese wines. The views from the granite walls of the 13th-century castle take in the huge man-made lake that has transformed the country-side. At dawn, the rising sun paints the water's surface a blaze of orange. The village's Igreja Matriz holds court over a maze of lanes lined with squat dwellings and restaurants.

8 Vila Nova de Milfontes

Tourist info: Rua António Mantas; (283) 996 599

This attractive town on the coast provides a welcome contrast from Alentejo's sun-parched interior. The old quarter is a hotchpotch of cobbled lanes and whitewashed cottages near a 16th-century sea fort, built to guard the town from pirates and buccaneers. The beaches – almost completely deserted out of season – are a popular summer attraction.

9 Elvas

Tourist info: Praça da República; (268) 622 236

Broad pentagonal bastions, star-shaped walls and gaping moats surround this busy frontier town near the Spanish border. The 17th-century military fortifications are among the finest in Europe and are listed as a UNESCO World Heritage Site. The battlements are best viewed from the late 15th-century castle. Elvas is also celebrated for the mighty Aqueduto da Amoreira and the outlying Forte de Santa Luzia and Forte da Graça.

Aqueduto da Amoreira in Elvas

10 Serpa

Tourist info: Rua dos Cavalos 19; (284) 544 727

This tranquil town is ideal for leisurely exploration. Start with the city walls and the stout towers of the Porta de Beja. Then discover the 17th-century aqueduct and noria. Within the walls, the castle provides the main focal point, and its ramparts offer sweeping views. Leave time to sample some *queijo Serpa* – a creamy ewe's milk cheese.

Porta de Beja in Serpa

A DAY IN ÉVORA

MORNING

Begin at the Praça do Giraldo and wander up Rua 5 de Outubro towards the Sé (cathedral). Look out for the 14th-century carved Apostles flanking the portal and, once inside, climb to the treasury to see the 13th-century ivory figure of the Virgin.

Adjacent to the cathedral is the Museu de Évora, where a dazzling 16th-century Flemish polyptych, *Life of the Virgin*, can be found upstairs.

On the opposite side of the square are the granite Corinthian columns of the Templo Romano – the best-preserved Roman monument in Portugal.

From here, retrace your steps back to Praça do Giraldo for lunch or a coffee and queijada de Évora at

Café Arcada *(Praça do Giraldo 7)*.

AFTERNOON

A few minutes' walk southeast from Praça do Giraldo is the impressive 16th-century Manueline-Gothic Igreja de São Francisco. The church's principal attraction is the eerie Capela dos Ossos (Bone Chapel), where the skeletal remains of some 5,000 monks line the walls and columns.

After this macabre experience, go back along Praça do Giraldo to Rota dos Vinhos do Alentejo for some wine-tasting. Alternatively, head outside the old town walls for the winery at **Adega Cartuxa** *(see p112)*. Arrive at 3pm or 4:30pm for a tour of this historic winery and the cellars.

See map on p106

The Best of the Rest

1 Cromlech of Almendres, Guadalupe

The Cromlech of Almendres stone circles are considered to be the most important megalith group in the Iberian peninsula. Nearby is the Neolithic Dolmen of Zambujeiro.

Cromlech of Almendres

2 Estremoz

The handcrafted clay figures of Estremoz are a spectacular find, declared as the Intangible Cultural Heritage of Humanity by UNESCO.

3 Crato

The Mosteiro de Flor da Rosa was once the headquarters of the 14th-century Order of Hospitaliers and is now a historic *pousada*. Exhibits in the Museu Municipal (closed Mon) explain more about Crato's illustrious past.

4 Arraiolos and Pavia

Arraiolos is celebrated for its handmade rugs; the Interpretation Centre in Praça do Município houses a fine collection. In Pavia, 18 km (11 miles) to the north, a tiny chapel has been built into a dolmen – something unique in Portugal.

5 Évoramonte

Dramatic views reward those who make it to Évoramonte's castle walls, which are embellished with curious stone "ropes". Dom Miguel famously ceded the throne here on 26 May 1834.

6 Viana do Alentejo

A little backwater famed for its natural springs, but also home to a fine 14th-century castle and a fortified church. To enjoy the vibrant Romaria a Cavalo festivities, arrive here on the last weekend of April.

7 Serra de São Mamede

This beautiful and diverse nature park is home to a stunning variety of wildlife: Bonelli's eagle, blue rock thrush, genet and the Iberian midwife toad are just some of the park's residents.

8 Portalegre

The superb Museu Guy Fino (closed Mon), named in honour of the founder of Portalegre's only remaining tapestry factory, showcases some of the finest examples of contemporary tapestry in Europe.

9 Redondo

Dozens of hole-in-the-wall *olarias* (pottery workshops) line the streets of Redondo – a great place to buy ceramic souvenirs.

10 Barragem de Alqueva

Europe's biggest artificial reservoir. A marina at Amieira runs houseboat sightseeing holidays, and there is a fine traditional restaurant.

Pretty Arraiolos

Places to Shop

1 Mercearia de Marvão, Marvão

Rua do Espírito Santo 1

A grocery, handicraft store and tavern all under the same roof, selling jams, cakes, honey, wines and liqueurs, as well as regional souvenirs crafted from local materials.

2 Mercearia Gadanha, Estremoz

Largo Dragões de Olivença 84

Stock up at this traditional deli with goat's and ewe's milk cheeses, olives, hams and the town's famous preserved plums. There is also a selection of teas and wines. The on-site restaurant is open for lunch and dinner.

Ewe's milk cheese from Mercearia Gadanha

3 Divinus Gourmet, Évora

Mercado Municipal de Évora, Praça 1 de Maio

A mouth-watering selection of more than 500 gourmet goodies, including chocolates, jams, pâtés and wines.

4 Coisas de Monsaraz, Monsaraz

Largo do Castelo 2

Homemade jams and other assorted knick-knacks can be bought from this little arts and crafts shop nestling in the shadows of the castle walls.

5 Terrius

Edifício Moinha da Cova, Portagem ■ www.terrius.pt

Focusing on regional produce, this splendid cultural and environmental centre also offers cookery and cork handicraft workshops.

6 Mercado Municipal, Vila Viçosa

Largo D. João IV ■ 9am–1pm daily

Housed in a modern complex in the town centre, Vila Viçosa's market is at its busiest early on Saturday mornings, when it overflows with fresh fruit and vegetables, and a wide selection of fish.

7 Portas de Mértola, Beja

This lively pedestrian zone is dotted with traditional shops and cafés, as well as places such as Maltesinhas and Café Luiz da Rocha.

8 Casa de Artesanato, Serpa

Rua dos Cavalos 33

A wonderfully atmospheric store packed full of hand-crafted goodies, including pots, shoes, handbags and blankets. The honey, cheeses, sausages and olive oil make lovely picnic ingredients.

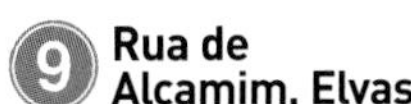

9 Rua de Alcamim, Elvas

A busy, attractive pedestrianized street with florists, music stores, shoe shops and the usual handicrafts. The weekly Monday market takes place near the impressive Aqueduto da Amoreira.

10 Rua 5 de Outubro, Évora

Lined with *artesanatos* (craft shops) selling ceramics, carved cork, copper *cataplanas* (cooking pots), hand-painted chairs and other curios. On the second Tuesday of every month an open-air market takes place across the Rossio de São Brás, outside the town walls.

Ceramics stall, Évora

See map on p106

Wineries

The expansive Adega Mayor vineyards

1 Herdade do Esporão

Herdade do Esporão, Reguengos de Monsaraz ■ (266) 509 280 ■ Visits 11am, 3pm ■ Advance booking required

Visit the vineyards, cellar and the Perdigões Archaeological Complex – a pre-historic monument.

2 Adega Cartuxa

Quinta de Valbom, Estrada da Soeira, Évora ■ (266) 748 383 ■ Visits 10:30am, 11:30am, 3pm & 4:30pm ■ Advance booking required

This historic winery is home to the celebrated Pêra-Manca. The old cellars house a wine press from 1776.

3 Herdade da Malhadinha Nova

Albernôa, Alentejo ■ (284) 965 210 ■ Jun–Sep: Visits 11am, noon, 3pm, 4pm & 5pm Mon–Sat; Oct–May: 11am, noon, 4pm & 5pm Mon–Sat ■ Advance booking required

Apart from touring the vineyards and cellars, visitors are encouraged to study the wine labels, which are designed by the owners' children.

4 Herdade dos Grous

Albernôa, Alentejo ■ (284) 960 000 ■ Visits 11am & 4pm daily ■ Advance booking required

A tour of the vineyard and winery is followed by tastings in the rustic bar.

5 João Portugal Ramos

Vila Santa, Estremoz ■ (268) 339 910 ■ Visits 9am–6:30pm Mon–Fri, 10am–6pm Sat (only for groups of 10 or more) ■ Advance booking required

Tours, lunch and tasting sessions are offered at this respected winery.

6 Adega Mayor

Herdade das Argamassas, Campo Maior ■ (268) 699 440 ■ Open 10am–1pm & 3–6pm daily ■ Advance booking required

This winery has a tasting room with views across a lake and over to Spain.

7 Cortes de Cima

Vidigueira, Alentejo ■ (284) 460 067 ■ Visits 10am & 6pm ■ Advance booking required

Guided tastings, accompanied by olive oil and bread, are held in a salon with views over the vineyards.

8 Herdade do Mouchão

Casa Branca Sousel, Portalegre Alentejo ■ (268) 530 210 ■ Open 8am–noon & 1–5pm Mon–Fri ■ Advance booking required

This *adega* has produced wine and *aguardente* brandy since the late 19th century. Facilities are quite limited.

9 Dona Maria

Quinta do Carmo, Estremoz ■ (268) 339 150 ■ Visits 10am & 5pm Sat ■ Advance booking required

This is a picturesque winery with an 18th-century chapel and gardens.

10 Adega José de Sousa

Rua de Mourão 1, Reguengos de Monsaraz, Alentejo ■ (266) 502 729 ■ Visits Apr–Oct: 10am, noon, 2:30pm & 5:30pm Mon–Sat; Nov–Mar: 10am, noon, 2:30pm & 4:30pm ■ Advance booking required

Famed for its astonishing clay amphorae cellar with a Romanesque ceiling, this is one of the world's most unusual wine cellars.

Places to Eat

PRICE CATEGORIES
For a three-course meal for one with half a bottle of wine (or equivalent meal), taxes and extra charges.

€ under €30 €€ €30–€50 €€€ over €50

1 Gadanha Mercearia

Largo Dragões de Olivença 84a, Estremoz ■ (268) 333 262 ■ Closed Mon ■ No veg dishes ■ €

This rustic eatery combines a restaurant and a wine shop, and also features a grocery store packed with regional goodies.

2 Restaurante Casa do Povo

Travessa do Chabouco, Marvão ■ (245) 993 160 ■ Closed Thu ■ No veg dishes ■ €

Sweeping terrace views and hearty portions of regional food in one of Portugal's most beautiful mountain villages makes dining here a treat.

Interior of Pousada Vila Viçosa

3 Pousada Vila Viçosa – D. João IV

Terreiro do Paço, Vila Viçosa ■ (268) 980 742 ■ €€

Be sure to opt for the regional menu at this beautiful former convent – dishes are based on the recipes of the nuns who used to live here.

4 A Pipa

Rua da Moeda 8, Beja ■ (284) 327 043 ■ Open noon–2:30pm & 7:30–10:30pm Mon–Sat ■ €

Grilled pork is a signature dish at this delightfully rustic restaurant.

5 Fialho

Travessa dos Mascarenhas 16, Évora ■ (266) 703 079 ■ Closed Mon, Jun & Jul ■ No veg dishes ■ €€

Local specialities include *cacão de coentrada* (dog fish with coriander sauce). Advance booking is essential.

6 Xarez

Rua de Santiago 33, Monsaraz ■ (266) 557 052 ■ Closed Jan, Wed D, Thu; D only in summer ■ No veg dishes ■ €

A menu of regional fare is served at this chic restaurant. It offers breathtaking views from the terrace.

7 Na Boca do Lobo

Ave Alexandre Herculano 20, Portalegre ■ (965) 416 630 ■ Closed Sun & Mon ■ €

Prepared by chef José Júlio, among the vast options of local fare, the menu includes *pernas da rã* (frog legs), a mouth-watering surprise.

8 Os Cucos

Mata Municipal, Vila Viçosa ■ (268) 980 806 ■ Closed 1–15 Aug ■ No veg dishes ■ €

Set in verdant, shady gardens, this eatery offers a daily menu, usually featuring earthy Alentejan fare. There is also an outside terrace.

9 Restaurante Alentejano

Praça da República, Serpa ■ (284) 544 335 ■ Closed Sun pm, Mon & Jul ■ No veg dishes ■ €

Order the *ensopado de borrego a pastora* (lamb stew, shepherd-ess style) for a real taste of the Alentejo.

10 Restaurante Panorâmico da Amieira

Amieira Marina, Amieira ■ (266) 611 175 ■ Apr–Oct: L Thu–Tue, D Fri–Sun; Nov–Mar: L Fri–Mon, D Fri–Sun ■ No veg dishes ■ €

Try to sit at a terrace table at this restaurant for views of the lake. Delicious Alentejo cuisine.

See map on p106 ←

Streetsmart

Traditional ceramics from Sagres

Getting Around

Arriving by Air

Lisbon, Porto and Faro are the main airports for long-haul flights into Portugal, while European budget airlines fly to cities across the country year-round at very reasonable prices. These budget European airlines also offer very good rates on regular internal flights within Portugal.

The most common entry and exit point for visitors to the Algarve by plane is **Faro International Airport**, which is located some 6 km (4 miles) west of the city centre. The airport serves both domestic and foreign carriers from all over Europe. Flights from the US and other trans-atlantic destinations route through Lisbon. Canadian carrier **Air Transat**, however, operates a direct Toronto–Faro service between late January and early April. Portugal's national airline, **TAP Portugal**, operates daily scheduled services between the cities of Faro, Lisbon and Porto.

Faro International Airport's website lists scheduled arrivals and departures. The airport has excellent public transport links into the city centre from the terminal. Local buses 14 and 16 run daily to the centre, departing every half an hour from 5am until 11pm. A taxi from the airport into the centre should cost around €14–16 and take approx-imately 20 minutes to half an hour.

International Train Travel

There are two main routes into Portugal by train. The famous Sud Express train departs daily at 6:45pm from Irun on the French–Spanish border, and splits near Coimbra, arriving into Lisbon and Porto. Irun can be reached from Austerlitz station in Paris. Travelling from London to Lisbon, using the **Eurostar** to reach Paris, and then the Sud Express to Lisbon, takes approximately 30 hours. Alternatively, the over-night train from Madrid takes 10 hours. Both routes are operated by the Spanish state-run service **Renfe**. You can purchase tickets online or at international train stations in Portugal. It is sensible to book ahead in peak season (Jul–Aug).

Regional Train Travel

As the largest city in the Algarve, Faro is the transportation hub for the region. **Faro Railway Station** is located on Largo da Estação, near the harbour. **Comboios de Portugal** (CP) operates all trains: the daily high-speed Alfa Pendular (AP) and intercity services (IC) from Lisbon, Porto and Braga terminate here.

Passengers can choose to travel *conforto* (first-class) or *turística* (second-class). Seat reservations are obligatory, although they are included in the ticket price. Faro is also on the Algarve rail line, which runs from Lagos in the west to Vila Real de Santo António on the Spanish border.

The regional railway line also connects Vila Real de Santo António with Lagos. While slow, the service is inexpensive and you can purchase a ticket onboard. If you plan to use the train regularly it may be worth purchasing a discounted 2-day (€20.90) or 3-day (€31.90) Tourist Travel Card, which allow unlimited rail travel within that their desig-nated time period. Both are available at larger train stations throughout the Algarve.

Long-Distance Bus Travel

Travelling to Portugal by coach is cheap but very time consuming. **Flixbus** offers a variety of routes into Portugal from many popular destinations in Western Europe, but it has long journey times.

There are excellent express coach services to the Algarve from cities across Portugal. The two main companies are **EVA Transportes** and **Rede Expressos**. Tickets can be purchased on the day of travel from bus stations and ticket desks, but it is prudent to book ahead, especially during the busy summer months.

Regional Bus Travel

The major coach companies operating in the Algarve are **Frota Azul Algarve**, Próximo and Eva. All operate fast and efficient regional services between the area's major coastal and inland towns. However, some rural bus travel is slow and schedules are sometimes unpredictable. Put your arm out to flag down an approaching bus, otherwise it won't stop. Note, bus stop signs *(paragem)* can be on the opposite side of the road, against the direction of intended travel.

Public Transport

In most urban areas bus services suffice as the sole means of public transport. Buses are run privately and several companies operate services between cities. However, most of the region's town and cities, including Faro, are fairly compact and most sights can be reached on foot.

Faro's main public transport provider **Próximo** operates an urban bus network linking the city centre with the airport, beach (Praia de Faro) and the various suburbs. Timetables, maps, fares, and safety and hygiene measures can be found online. Be aware that many routes do not operate in the evenings or at weekends.

To travel beyond Faro's city limits, hop on one of the regional bus services *(see p116)*, which provide reliable transportation throughout the Algarve for a reasonable price.

Tickets

Tickets for AP and IC trains can usually be booked up to 30 days ahead, and considerable discounts can be enjoyed on advance purchase (at least five days) and return tickets. There are also additional 50 per cent discounts for children aged 5–12 (under-5s go free) and for passengers aged 65 and over. Students with valid youth cards also receive discounts.

If a regional rail station is unstaffed you can pay the ticket inspector on board for your ticket. To benefit from any travel discounts you will need to show proof of identity. You can book long-distance tickets online or buy them at bus stations, but they cannot be purchased directly from the driver. Increasingly, digital tickets are being issued to mobile devices. EVA Transportes has a 3-day (€30.50) and a 7-day (€38.20) Tourist Pass for unlimited travel in the Algarve on its extensive bus network.

Taxi

A relatively inexpensive travel option, taxis are widely used in the Algarve. The starting rate for a taxi hailed in the street or flagged at a rank is €3.25. If you phone for a cab an extra 80 cents is levied. Additional charges will be made for carrying luggage, and rates increase by 25 per cent from 9pm to 6am, at weekends and on public holidays. Charges are posted inside the taxi. Note that it is not always cost-effective to travel short distances, because tariffs are usually fixed. Outside towns, journeys by taxi are per kilometre, so establish a price beforehand. Tipping is discretionary, though adding 5–10 per cent to the fare is the norm. The Faro International Airport website has a taxi-service operation page.

DIRECTORY

ARRIVING BY AIR

Air Transat
W airtransat.com

Faro International Airport
MAP K6 ■ 8001-701 Faro
T (289) 800 800
W aeroportofaro.pt

TAP Portugal
W flytap.com

INTERNATIONAL TRAIN TRAVEL

Eurostar
W eurostar.com

Renfe
W renfe.com

REGIONAL TRAIN TRAVEL

Comboios de Portugal
W cp.pt

Faro Railway Station
MAP K6 ■ Largo de Estação, Faro
T (707) 210 220

LONG-DISTANCE BUS TRAVEL

EVA Transportes
W eva-bus.com

Flixbus
W global.flixbus.com

Rede Expressos
W rede-expressos.pt

REGIONAL BUS TRAVEL

Frota Azul Algarve
W frotazul-algarve.pt

PUBLIC TRANSPORT

Próximo
W próximo.pt

Driving

A car is by far the most convenient way to see all that the Algarve has to offer, and it allows you more freedom to explore the region on your own terms without relying on bus or train services.

Portugal's comprehensive motorway system allows for speedy travel between major cities, although less-travelled rural roads may be in need of repair. Make sure you are familiar with the rules of the road and carry all necessary documentation with you at all times.

A tolled motorway (A2) links Portugal's capital, Lisbon, with the Algarve. Tickets are issued from toll booths when you join a motorway and can be redeemed at the next booth, or when you leave. The cost depends on the distance travelled and vehicle class. Do not use the Via Verde lane at tolls; this is only for drivers who subscribe to an electronic pre-payment system.

Unless you exit at São Bartolomeu de Messines (junction 14), continuing on the A2 south will bring you onto the A22 motorway (Via do Infante). This is an electronically tolled highway and number-plate-recognition cameras are used to charge. If you are driving your own vehicle you have three different ways of paying. The **Portugal Tolls** website details the methods. If using a hire car you need to pay for road usage at a post office: quote your registration number to find out how much you owe. Some rental-car companies have fitted their fleets with transponders to automatically record travel on the A22. Upon return of the vehicle, your credit card will be charged the applicable fee.

An alternative way to drive to the Algarve is to use the IC1. Though slower, the road is more scenic and avoids the tolled A2. The A49 from Huelva in Spain crosses the bridge over the Rio Guadiana to merge with the A22 near the town of Vila Real de Santo António.

Rules of the Road

When driving a vehicle in Portugal, drive on the right and use the left lane only for passing other vehicles. The wearing of seat belts is required for all passengers regardless of age, and heavy fines are incurred if you are caught using a mobile phone while driving.

The speed limit is 50 km/h (35 mph) in towns and villages, 90 km/h (60 mph) on normal roads and 120 km/h (80 mph) on motorways. Drivers are legally required to stop at pedestrian crossings. The blood-alcohol concentration (BAC) limit is 0.5mg/ml and is very strictly enforced. Dashboard cameras are illegal in Portugal; they contravene privacy laws.

Drivers should always carry their passport, licence and insurance details. In the event of an accident or breakdown, the driver and passengers must don a fluorescent yellow safety vest and erect a collapsible warning triangle 50 m (164 ft) behind the vehicle. The law stipluates that both of these items must be stored in the trunk of the vehicle at all times.

The local motoring association, the **ACP** (Automóvel Club de Portugal), has a reciprocal breakdown service with most other international motoring organizations. To qualify, drivers should take out European cover with their own organization. Should you be involved in an accident, the emergency services number is 112. If you have simply broken down, call the ACP or, if driving a hired car, check the instructions supplied by your chosen company.

Driver's licences issued by any EU member state are valid throughout the EU, including Portugal. If visiting from outside the EU, you may need to apply for an International Driving Permit (IDP). If you are stopped by the police, your personal ID or passport, driving licence and insurance policy will be requested. Proof of ownership may also be needed if it is your own vehicle.

Car Rental

Hiring a car is a popular option. Car hire agencies can be found in main towns and at airports. To rent a car in Portugal you must be over 18 and have held a valid licence for at least one year, although those under 25 usually need to pay a surcharge. Prices drop considerably in the low season and some companies offer special off-peak and weekend deals. It is wise to arrange third-party insurance beforehand or take the pricier "no excess" insurance deals offered upon pick-up. Most car hire companies give the option to pay all road toll fees upon the vehicle's return.

Scooter and Bicycle Hire

Scooters are suitable for short journeys only; inter-city travel really requires a motorcycle. Most rental companies require a deposit and ask that you leave your passport at the rental shop. You must have a driver's licence valid for your desired bike category. 50cc vehicles are forbidden on motorways and all riders must wear helmets by law.

The Algarve's historic town centres are ill-equipped for bicycles, but popular cycling routes exist on the flatter fringes and you can rent bicycles in most urban areas and touristic centres. It is best to attempt long-distance journeys during the milder shoulder seasons when the roads are quieter and the heat is much more manageable.

Walking and Hiking

With a vast network of trails, such as the 300-km (186-mile) Via Algarviana (GR13) connecting Alcoutim to Cabo de São Vicente, the Algarve is a fantastic destination for walkers and hikers, but planning and good preparation are essential. Ensure you have good walking boots, suitable clothing and plenty of water, especially if you plan to be out in the heat of the day. Always tell someone where you're going and when you plan to return.

Trips and Tours

City Sightseeing operates hop-on hop-off, open-top bus tours in and around Albufeira. The buses stop at all the main sights, including the beach. Fun-packed jeep safaris are organized by **Algarve Jeep Safari**, and travel well off the beaten track. The more adventurous can take the wheel in one of their buggies.

Algarve Online arranges tours and excursions by private coach to all areas of the region, plus extended journeys to other parts of Portugal and southern Spain.

Formosamar arranges activities that are certified as Ecotourism by the Portuguese Institute for Conservation of Nature and Biodiversity. The company promotes the natural and cultural heritage of the Ria Formosa area.

Renting a Segway from **Algarve by Segway** provides a novel way of sightseeing. Tour options include a trip to the peak of Fóia *(see p20)*.

The Mountain Bike Adventure has qualified guides that lead expeditions over some of Europe's finest tracks.

An unusual way to roam the region is by motorized rickshaw. **Love Tuk Olhão** combines city tours with excursions to the nearby Parque Natural da Ria Formosa *(see pp30–33)*.

Nature enthusiasts, meanwhile, can enjoy a boat trip with **Natura Algarve** and sail alongside dolphins. The River Guadiana is the backdrop for trips organized by **Fun River**. The company also arranges heritage-themed walks and bicycle rides.

DIRECTORY

DRIVING

Portugal Tolls
W portugaltolls.com

RULES OF THE ROAD

ACP
W acp.pt
T 808 502 502

TRIPS AND TOURS

Algarve Jeep Safari
W algarvejeepsafari.com

Algarve Online
W algarve-tours-excursions.com

Algarve by Segway
W algarvebysegway.com

City Sightseeing
W city-sightseeing.com

Formosamar
W formosamar.com

Fun River
W fun-river.com

Love Tuk Olhão
W lovetukolhao.pt

The Mountain Bike Adventure
W themountainbikeadventure.com

Natura Algarve
W natura-algarve.com

Practical Information

Passports and Visas

For entry requirements, including visas, consult your nearest Portuguese embassy or check the Portuguese **Ministry of Foreign Affairs**. EU nationals and citizens of the UK, US, Canada, Australia and New Zealand do not need visas for stays of up to three months; non-EU nationals must have passports valid for at least three months beyond their planned departure date.

Government Advice

Now more than ever, it is important to consult both your and the Portuguese government's advice before travelling. The **UK Foreign and Common-wealth Office**, the **US State Department**, the **Australian Department of Foreign Affairs and Trade** and the **Câmara Municipal de Lisboa** offer the latest information on security, health and local regulations.

Customs Information

You can find information on the laws relating to goods and currency taken in or out of Portugal on the **Visit Portugal** website.

For EU citizens, there are no limits on goods taken into or out of the country, provided they are for your personal use.

Insurance

We recommend that you take out a comprehensive insurance policy covering theft, loss of belongings, medical care, cancell-ations and delays, and read the small print.

UK citizens are eligible for free emergency medical care in Portugal provided they have a valid EHIC (European Health Insurance Card) or GHIC (UK Global Health Insurance Card). All other nationalities should make sure to take out private health insurance.

Health

Portugal has a world-class health system. Emergency medical care is free for all EU citizens. If you have an EHIC, present this as soon as possible. You may have to pay after treatment and reclaim the money later. For other visitors, pay-ment of hospital and other medical expenses is the patient's responsibility. It is therefore important to arrange comprehensive medical insurance before you travel.

The Algarve has three hospitals: **Hospital de Faro, Lagos Hospital** and **Portimão Hospital**. Hospital de Faro is the largest facility and offers *urgência* (emergency) services. If you require medical assistance for minor injuries, you should go to the local *centro da saúde* (health centre).

Farmácias (pharmacies) are easily identifiable by their green cross sign. **SmartExpat** provides useful information regarding healthcare for visitors in Portugal. No vaccinations are required to enter the country.

Smoking, Drugs and Alcohol

Smoking is banned in enclosed public spaces and is a fineable offence.

Portugal has a high alcohol consumption rate, however it is frowned upon to be openly drunk. It is common for locals to drink outside bars on the street.

All drugs are decriminalized in Portugal, but possession of small quantities is considered a public health issue and results in a warning or small fine.

ID

By law you must carry ID with you at all times. A photocopy of your passport should suffice. If stopped by the police you may be asked to report to a police station with the original document.

Personal Security

The Algarve enjoys a reputation as a safe and peaceful destination. Violent crime is very rare. However, petty theft is a problem in the holiday resorts during the crowded summer months. If you have anything stolen, report the crime within 24 hours to the nearest police station and take ID with you. Get a copy of the crime report to make an insurance claim. Visitors can report assaults, thefts and lost property to a dedicated unit, **Police**

Support Services for Tourists. The number to dial in an **emergency** is 112. Ask for the required service – *polícia* (police), *ambulância* (ambulance) or *bombeiros* (fire brigade)

The Portuguese are generally accepting of all people, regardless of their race, gender or sexuality. Homosexuality was legalized in 1982 and in 2010, Portugal became the eighth country in the world to recognize same-sex marriage. If you do feel unsafe, the **Safe Space Alliance** pinpoints your nearest refuge.

Travellers with Specific Requirements

Steep hills and narrow cobbled streets can prove a challenge for visitors with reduced mobility. Facilities have improved over recent years, with increased wheelchair access, adapted toilets and reserved car parking. There are ramps and lifts in many public places and on public transport. Most sights offer audio guides for the visually impaired and audio induction loops for the hard of hearing.

MyWay is an excellent support service for air passengers with limited mobility. The service must be pre-booked with the air carrier when reserving the flight. Passengers are assisted with luggage and are escorted to and from their aircraft seat. At Faro International Airport, look for the designated MyWay service points.

Tour companies, such as **Tourism For All** offer specialist packages, while **Accessible Portugal** is a Lisbon-based travel agency with English-speaking staff that operates throughout Portugal. Specializing in arranging holidays for those with special needs, it arranges transfers by vehicles adapted for carrying wheelchairs. It also gives comprehensive advice on travelling with limited mobility and it has created a website and app called **TUR4all** which promotes accessible tourism in Portugal. **Portugal 4All Senses,** meanwhile, organizes tours with the visually impaired in mind.

Faro-based **Algarve Accessible** publishes a list of wheelchair-friendly accommodation and attractions, and offers mobility aids for hire.

DIRECTORY

PASSPORTS AND VISAS

Ministry of Foreign Affairs
W vistos.mne.gov.pt

GOVERNMENT ADVICE

Australian Department of Foreign Affairs and Trade
W smartraveller.gov.au

Câmara Municipal de Lisboa
W visitar.lisboa.pt

UK Foreign and Commonwealth Office
W gov.uk/foreign-travel-advice

US Department of State
W travel.state.gov

CUSTOMS INFORMATION

Visit Portugal
W visitportugal.com

HEALTH

Hospital de Faro
MAP K6
Rua Leão Penedo
T (289) 891 100
W hdfaro.min-saude.pt

Lagos Hospital
MAP D5
Rua Castelo dos Governadores
T (282) 770 100

Portimão Hospital
MAP E4
Sítio do Poço Seco
T (282) 450 300

SmartExpat
W smartexpat.com

PERSONAL SECURITY

Emergency Services
T 112

Police Support Services For Tourists
Albufeira Police
T (289) 513 203
Tourist Help Line
T (808) 781 212
Vilamoura Police
T (289) 381 780

Safe Space Alliance
W safespacealliance.com

TRAVELLERS WITH SPECIFIC REQUIREMENTS

Accessible Portugal
T (926) 910 989
W accessibleportugal.com

Algarve Accessible
T (289) 810 100
W algarve-accessible.com

MyWay
T (289) 800 800
W flytap.com/en-pt/special-needs/my-way

Portugal 4All Senses
W portugal4allsenses.pt

Tourism For All
W tourism-for-all.com

TUR4all
W tur4all.pt

Time Difference

Portugal operates on Greenwich Mean Time (GMT), which is four hours ahead of Eastern Standard Time (EST). Clocks go forward an hour in late March and back in late October.

Money

Portugal is one of the European countries using the euro (€). Major credit cards are widely accepted in bigger hotels, shops, restaurants and bars. Contactless payments are gradually becoming more common, but it's always a good idea to carry cash for smaller items, public transport and taxi fares. The easiest way to withdraw money is to use ATMs, known as Multibanco, which are widely available. Nearly all accept debit and credit cards from the major card companies, but transaction charges will apply.

Tipping around 10 per cent is normal when dining out or travelling by taxi; hotel porters and house-keeping will expect €1-2 per bag or day.

Electrical Appliances

Portugal uses two-pin plugs (220–240 volts). You will need an adaptor, and possibly a transformer (for some US appliances).

Mobile Phones and Wi-Fi

Most mobile phones have good connections throughout the Algarve. Visitors travelling to Portugal with EU tariffs are able to use their devices abroad without being impacted by hefty roaming charges. Users will be charged the same rates for data, calls and texts as they would do at home. Portugal's country dialling code is 351.

Free Wi-Fi is not yet widespread in Portugal, but it can be found in hotels, restaurants and bars, specifically those aimed at tourists.

Postal Services

The postal service is CTT Correios de Portugal. Post offices *(correios)* are usually open weekdays 9am–6pm. Some larger branches are also open on Saturday mornings. Firstclass mail is known as *correio azul* and second-class mail is called *normal*. Stamps are available from post offices or any shop displaying a *Correios* sign.

Weather

The Algarve enjoys a typical Mediterranean climate with long, warm and dry summers and mild winters. The region receives more sun each year than California. Average daytime temperatures in summer hover between 24°C (75°F) and 29°C (84°F). In winter it rarely drops below 15°C (60°F), though inland it can become chilly. Spring and autumn are the best times to visit if you want to avoid the crowds that flock here in the hottest months: July and August.

Opening Hours

Generally, the Algarve's main shopping hours are 9am–1pm and 3–7pm, Mon–Fri. Most are also open all day Saturday from 9am–7pm in high season. Hours are often extended in coastal resorts during summer, and Sunday trading is commonplace. Shopping centres and malls are open seven days a week until midnight.

Normal banking hours are 8:30am–3pm, Mon–Fri. Some larger branches in the Algarve are also open in the evenings during the summer months. Likewise, bureaux de change and financial services companies usually operate flexible hours to take advantage of the seasonal influx of tourists.

Museums, monuments, galleries and some churches tend to regulate their own visiting times, but are nearly always closed on Mondays as well as on Christmas Day, New Year's Day, and during Easter and other public holidays. As a rule, though, historic visitor attractions are open 10am–5pm Tue–Sun, with many establishments closing for lunch either at noon–2pm or at 12:30–2:30pm.

COVID-19

The pandemic continues to affect Portugal. Some museums, tourist attractions and hospitality venues are operating on reduced or temporary opening hours, and require visitors to make advance bookings for a specific date and time. Always check ahead before visiting.

Visitor Information

The **Visit Portugal** website offers a general overview of the region, though the **Turismo do Algarve** site provides more detailed information.

There is a tourist office in every major town across the region. Here you will find maps, brochures, pamphlets, accommodation tips and the tourist board's free monthly *Algarve Guide*.

Hotel receptions are a good source of visitor information, and guests can often enjoy discounts if they book an attraction via staff at the front desk.

The region's beaches are some of the best in Europe. Beachgoers should note that a red flag hoisted over the sand indicates a strong tide or dangerous undertow, and swimming is prohibited. A yellow flag signifies caution – you should stay within your depth. When a green flag is flying, the water is safe. Nasty stings in shallow water may be from poisonous weever fish *(peixe-aranha)* buried in the sand. In the event of a sting, seek the help of a lifeguard or apply hot water to the area, which can alleviate the intense pain and swelling.

Visiting Churches and Cathedrals

Most churches and cathedrals will not permit visitors during Sunday Mass. Generally, entrance is free; however a fee may apply to enter special areas, like cloisters.

Many areas are deeply religious, particularly those away from the main tourist hubs. When visiting religious buildings ensure that knees and shoulders are covered.

Local Customs

Portugal retains a very strong Catholic identity. Be respectful when visiting religious sites or attending religious events.

A much-loved aspect of Portugal is the slow pace of life. Avoid impatience as a pedestrian, at events and when making social engagements.

Language

Portuguese is the official language. English is usually widely spoken in most large towns, cities and tourist resorts, but the same cannot always be said for rural areas.

Taxes and Refunds

VAT is usually 23 per cent. Under certain conditions, non-EU citizens can claim a rebate. You can claim before you buy (show your passport to the shop assistant and complete a form) or retrospectively by presenting a customs officer with your receipts as you leave.

Accommodation

There is an outstanding range of accommodation in the Algarve, from luxury resort hotels to hostels, self-catering apartments to farmhouses. There are also restored palaces and sea forts to consider, golf and country clubs, boutique boltholes and excellent campsites. Prices vary, depending on the season. Room rates are obviously higher during the summer months and at peak travel periods such as the Easter period, and often on Friday and Saturday nights. Prices tend to plummet considerably during the winter months. Booking directly with the hotel online is usually the best way to arrange your stay, and many upmarket hotel websites feature offers and promotions to guests who do so. Good, budget options include staying in a one-star hotel, classified as a *pensão* or *residencial*. These offer clean, value-for-money facilities and may provide meals or offer breakfast. You can also rent a room in a private house, known as a *quarto* – look out for signs in windows, or check with the local tourist office.

Pousadas de Juventude operates several youth hostels in the region. **Pousadas de Portugal** has three hotels in the Algarve. These are beautiful and historic properties offering luxury accommodation.

DIRECTORY

VISITOR INFORMATION

Turismo do Algarve
W visitalgarve.pt

Visit Portugal
W visitportugal.com

ACCOMMODATION

Pousadas de Juventude
W pousadasjuventude.pt

Pousadas de Portugal
W pestana.com

Places to Stay

PRICE CATEGORIES

For a standard, double room per night (with breakfast if included), taxes and extra charges.

€ under €100 €€ €100–300 €€€ over €300

Luxury, Five-Star Hotels

Anantara Vilamoura Algarve Resort

MAP H5 ■ Avenida dos Descobrimentos, Vilamoura ■ (289) 317 000 ■ www.anantara.com ■ €€

Overlooking the Oceânico Victoria golf course *(see p60)*, this modern and attractive property boasts three pools and a tennis court among its premium guest facilities.The therapists at the Elements Spa by Banyan Tree deliver an authentic Oriental spa experience. Among the massages available is the Balinese massage, which stimulates circulation, increases energy flow and alleviates tension.

Cascade Wellness & Lifestyle Resort

MAP D5 ■ Praia do Canavial, Lagos ■ (282) 771 500 ■ www.cascaderesortalgarve.com ■ €€€

Located on a secluded clifftop, all rooms and suites enjoy either pool or ocean views. Amenities include a spa, a golf academy, tennis courts and the Senses restaurant.

Conrad Algarve

MAP J5 ■ Estrada do Quinta do Largo, Quinta do Largo ■ (289) 350 700 ■ www.conradalgarve.com ■ €€€

Top-notch contemporary design and use of the latest technology define this exceptional property. Amenities include the Michelin-starred restaurant Gusto a spa, indoor and outdoor swimming pools, a children's club and nearby championship golf courses.

Hotel Quinta do Lago

MAP J5 ■ Quinta do Lago, near Almancil ■ (289) 350 350 ■ www.hotelquintadolago.com ■ €€€

Overlooking Ria Formosa lagoon and the ocean, this sophisticated resort has two excellent restaurants: the Brisa do Mar (traditional Portuguese cuisine) and Cá d'Oro (famed for its Italian gastronomy). Leisure facilities include a golf course and a health club with a gym and sauna.

Vila Joya Boutique Resort

MAP G5 ■ Praia da Galé, Albufeira ■ (289) 591 795 ■ www.vilajoya.com ■ €€€

An exclusive gourmet retreat, with splendid seafront gardens and a two-starred Michelin restaurant *(see p71)*. Spa facilities and Ayurvedic massage are available.

Vila Vita Parc Resort & Spa

MAP F5 ■ Alporchinhos, Porches, Armação de Pêra ■ (282) 310 100 ■ www.vilavitaparc.com ■ €€€

At this luxury clifftop resort set above a secluded beach, Moorish-inspired architecture is complemented by contemporary flourishes. Guest amenities include the Vital Spa, an 18-hole putting green and a kids' park. The Ocean Restaurant has two Michelin stars *(see p71)*.

Spa Hotels and Resorts

Hilton Vilamoura As Cascatas Golf Resort & Spa

MAP H5 ■ Rua da Torre d'Agua, Vilamoura ■ (289) 304 000 ■ www.hiltonvilamouraresort.com.pt ■ €€

Portugal's largest spa, 7 Seven Spa, is located here. Hydro-massage pools, ice fountains and aromatic steam baths exemplify the resort's aquatic theme. The invigorating water tunnel experience is a favourite option for guests. Treatments include a detox bath and a body wrap with sculpting massage.

Real Marina Hotel & Spa

MAP L5 ■ Avenida 5 de Outubro, Olhão ■ (289) 091 300 ■ www.realmarina.realhotelsgroup.com ■ €€

The hydrotherapy treatments at the Real Spa Therapy are highly regarded and are offered as baths, wraps and massages. There are nine treatment rooms, and facilities include a Turkish bath, a sauna and a Vichy shower. The spa has wonderful views over the Ria Formosa.

Bela Vista Hotel & Spa

MAP E5 ■ Avenida Tomás Cabreira, Praia da Rocha ■ (282) 460 280 ■ www.hotelbelavista.net ■ €€€

Branded by L'Occitane, the boutique spa uses some of the region's traditions in its massage techniques: the "Ritual de Amêndoa Algarvia", for example, includes an exfoliation using almond paste. It also houses the Michelin-starred Vista Restaurant.

Epic Sana Algarve

MAP G5 ■ Olhos de Água, Albufeira ■ (289) 104 300 ■ www.algarve.epic.sanahotels.com ■ €€€

Guests can have massages and treatments in a garden pavilion at this modern oceanfront resort. The Sayanna Wellness experience also embraces an intoxicating variety of treatments designed by Aromatherapy Associates. Fitness retreats and boot camps can be arranged.

Pine Cliffs Resort

MAP G5 ■ Praia da Falésia, Albufeira ■ (289) 500 300 ■ www.pinecliffs.com ■ €€€

At 1000 sq m (3,300 sq ft), the Destination SPA serves the entire resort, including the Pine Cliffs Ocean Suites. The state-of-the-art facility, one of the newest in the Algarve, encompasses 11 treatment rooms and the impressive Spa Suite.

Vilalara Thalassa Resort

MAP F5 ■ Praia das Gaivotas, Lagoa ■ (282) 320 000 ■ www. vilalararesort.com ■ €€€

Vilalara features one of the world's finest thalassotherapy (sea-water bathing) centres, as well as an extensive range of facilities and treatments for health, beauty and wellbeing. Two excellent restaurants on-site.

Resort Hotels for Families

Grande Real Santa Eulália Resort & Hotel Spa

MAP G5 ■ Praia de Santa Eulália, Albufeira ■ (289) 598 000 ■ www.granderealsantaeulaliahotel.com ■ €€

This five-star resort has direct beach access and offers pampering at its Real Spa Thalasso. Baby-sitting is offered with advance notice, and children can try activities at the complimentary children's club.

Hotel Algarve Casino

MAP E5 ■ Avenida Tomás Cabreira, Praia da Rocha ■ (282) 402 000 ■ www.gruposolverde.pt ■ €€

This offers the complete family holiday package. Apart from the famous Praia da Rocha beach, leisure facilities on hand include a swimming pool, a video room, a children's zone and a casino that stages cabaret.

Hotel Belavista da Luz

MAP C5 ■ Praia da Luz, Lagos ■ (282) 788 655 ■ www.belavistadaluz.com ■ €€

A family-run hotel, built in a horseshoe shape to enclose two inviting pools and a "children's zone". Golf, horse riding, walking tours and scuba diving can be organized by staff.

Hotel Dom Pedro Marina

MAP H5 ■ Rua Tivoli, Vilamoura ■ (289) 300 780 ■ www.dompedro.com ■ €€

With its own exclusive beach area next to Vilamoura marina, this is a popular choice. Childcare is available, and facilities for adults include pools and a restaurant specializing in fine Italian cuisine.

Pestana Alvor Park

MAP D5 ■ Quinta do Ribeiro, Alvor ■ (282) 000 500 ■ www.pestana.com ■ €€

An attractive aparthotel and villa complex. Its facilities include indoor and outdoor pools, a sauna, gym and a games room. A children's fun centre is complemented by nearby golf, tennis and watersports facilities.

Vila Galé Albacora

MAP M4 ■ Quatro Águas, Tavira ■ (281) 380 800 ■ www.vilagale.com ■ €€

A children's club and entertainment, plus two swimming pools, a diving centre and the wonderful beaches at Ilha de Tavira make this hotel perfect for families.

The Lake Spa Resort

MAP H5 ■ Praia da Falésia, Vilamoura ■ (289) 320 700 ■ www.thelakeresort.com ■ €€€

One of the pools here is designed as a shallow lake with a sandy beach. Spacious apartments are available, and there is a spa and three restaurants. Baby-sitting services are available, and youngsters can enjoy the activities at the Koala Club.

Martinhal Beach Resort & Hotel

MAP B6 ■ Quinta do Martinhal, near Sagres ■ (282) 240 200 ■ www.martinhal.com ■ €€€

Ideal for families with children of all ages, this resort offers spacious and stylishly designed accommodation. The restaurants and spa are also family-friendly. The fashionable hotel section is more suited to couples.

Boutique Places to Stay

Aldeia da Pedralva

MAP B4 ■ Pedralva, north of Vila do Bispo ■ (282) 639 342 ■ No air conditioning ■ www.aldeiadapedralva.com ■ €€

An entire country village has been carefully restored to offer self-catering stays in wonderfully authentic whitewashed cottages overlooking pretty countryside. Members of staff are all friendly and helpful, and there is also a handy shop and an on-site bar and restaurant.

Fazenda Nova Country House

MAP M4 ■ Estiramentens, Santo Estevão ■ (281) 961 913 ■ www.fazendanova.eu ■ €€

Set in a pretty valley, this British-run Portuguese country house has self-contained apartments and ten large suites – nine with a private garden or terrace. Traditional architecture is combined with fresh and contemporary interior design, and the grounds are delightful.

Forte de São João da Barra

MAP N4 ■ Barroca, Cabanas ■ (960) 375 419 ■ No air conditioning ■ www.fortesaojoaodabarra.com ■ €€

This beautifully refurbished and secluded 17th-century fort overlooks the crystal-blue lagoons of the Ria Formosa. The grounds incorporate a plunge pool. Call for directions.

Pousada de Tavira – Convento da Graça

MAP M4 ■ Rua D. Paio Peres Correia, Tavira ■ (281) 329 040 ■ www.pousadas.pt ■ €€

Housed in a stunningly refurbished, 16th-century convent replete with cloisters, the pousada's modern rooms overlook a pool and the old town walls. Guest amenities include the Magic Wellness centre and a notable Portuguese restaurant.

Quinta das Achadas

MAP D4 ■ Estrada da Barragem, Odiáxere ■ (282) 798 425 ■ No air conditioning ■ www.algarveholiday.net ■ €€

This refurbished family-run farmhouse is set in wonderful gardens on a tranquil, 3-hectare site. There is a swimming pool, an outdoor Jacuzzi and a children's play area. A communal dinner is prepared twice a week.

Quinta do Caracol

MAP M4 ■ Rua de São Pedro, Tavira ■ (281) 322 475 ■ www.quintadocaracol.com ■ €€

A 17th-century farm that has been converted into a series of beautiful apartments, each named after flowers. Birdsong from the garden aviary drifts through the outdoor dining areas.

Vila Valverde Design & Country House

MAP C5 ■ Estrada da Praia da Luz, Valverde ■ (282) 790 790 ■ No disabled access ■ www.vilavalverde.com ■ €€

A boutique hotel with 15 individually decorated rooms. Amenities include heated indoor and outdoor pools, plus a fitness centre.

Quinta Bonita

MAP D5 ■ Matos Morenos, Quatro Estradas, near Lagos ■ (282) 762 135 ■ www.quintabonitaalgarve.com ■ €€€

Embedded in landscaped grounds, this peaceful retreat combines traditional character with luxurious boutique flourishes. There is an enticing outside pool.

Hotels with Golf Courses

Amendoeira Golf Resort

MAP F4 ■ Morgado da Lameira ■ (282) 320 820 ■ www.amendoeiraresort.com ■ €€

Fully equipped, self-catering apartments and villas with pools. The clubhouse features a restaurant and a golf academy, and overlooks the Faldo and O'Connor Jnr layouts. A free shuttle bus to the beach operates in July and August.

Morgado Golf & Country Club

MAP E4 ■ Morgado do Reguengo ■ (282) 241 540 ■ www.nauhotels.com ■ €€

All 98 rooms at this stylish hotel overlook

the Morgado Golf Course. Guests have the use of four swimming pools, and a kid's club functions between July and September. Views from the restaurant and bars take in the region's rustic hinterland.

Penina Hotel & Golf Resort

MAP E4 ■ Penina, near Portimão ■ (282) 420 200 ■ www.penina.com ■ €€
Guests at this luxury resort can enjoy the use of the 18-hole, Sir Henry Cotton layout, which has hosted the Portuguese Open several times. There are also two 9-hole courses *(see p60)*.

Pestana Vila Sol Golf & Resort

MAP J5 ■ Morgadinhos, near Vilamoura ■ (289) 320 320 ■ www.pestana.com ■ €€
A renowned 18-hole Championship golf course designed by architect Donald Steel meanders around this five-star resort via several exciting water features.

Dona Filipa & San Lorenzo Golf Resort

MAP J5 ■ Vale do Lobo, Almancil ■ (289) 357 200 ■ www.donafilipahotel.com ■ €€€
This resort offers five-star accommodation, and priority of play at the par 72 scenic masterpiece is offered to hotel guests.

Monte Rei Golf & Country Club

MAP N4 ■ Sítio do Pocinho, Sesmarias ■ (281) 950 950 ■ www.monte-rei.com ■ €€€
Short-term villa rentals at this serene country club make it ideal for small groups or families. Exclusive leisure amenities include swimming pools, tennis courts, a spa and fine dining. There is also the peerless Jack Nicklaus-designed championship golf course *(see p61)*.

Pine Cliffs Hotel

MAP G5 ■ Praia da Falésia, Albufeira ■ (289) 500 100 ■ www.pinecliffs.com ■ €€€
The hotel has a spectacular clifftop course *(see p60)*. The course and luxury hotel form the hub of the exclusive Pine Cliffs resort.

Mid-Range Hotels

Eurotel Altura

MAP P4 ■ Avenida 24 de Junho, Altura ■ (281) 956 450 ■ www.eurotel-altura.com ■ €€
With a perfect location by the ocean, this smart, family-friendly resort offers rooms that face the ocean. Facilities include a wellness center, spa, tennis court and a children's club. The Quinta da Ria golf course is nearby.

Hotel Eva

MAP K6 ■ Avenida da República, 1, Faro ■ (289) 001 000 ■ www.ap-hotelsresorts.com ■ €€
Hotel Eva is very comfortable and conveniently situated right on Faro's marina. The panorama from the rooftop swimming pool is outstanding and takes in the Ria Formosa. The city's historic old quarter is a 5-minute walk away.

Hotel Jupiter

MAP E5 ■ Avenida Tomás Cabreira 92, Praia da Rocha ■ (282) 470 470 ■ www.jupiteralgarvehotel.com ■ €€
Superbly appointed throughout, Hotel Jupiter's beachfront accommodation includes "Deluxe" rooms, which enjoy majestic ocean views. An excellent spa offers a hydrotherapy circuit, among other treatments. There is a fitness room and indoor and outdoor pools (covered over in winter). The restaurant serves delicious regional cuisine.

Hotel Termal, Villa Termal das Caldas de Monchique Spa Resort

MAP E3 ■ Caldas de Monchique ■ (282) 910 910 ■ www.monchiquetermalresort.com ■ €€
One of five hotel options within the Villa Termal das Caldas de Monchique Spa Resort, Hotel Termal's 36 "Essencial" rooms are classically styled and afford pleasing views over the gardens and surrounding woodland.

Memmo Baleeira

MAP B6 ■ Sítio da Baleeira, Sagres ■ (282) 624 212 ■ www.memmohotels.com ■ €€
Memmo's stylish rooms enjoy picturesque garden and harbour views. Facilities include an excellent restaurant, spa, gym and a pool. There is also a surf centre where outdoor activities can be booked. Reservations are recommended for August.

***For a key to hotel price categories** see p124*

Porto Bay Falésia

MAP H5 ■ Quinta do Milharo, near Olhas de Agua ■ (289) 007 700 ■ www.portobay.com ■ €€
Overlooking the picturesque Praia da Falésia *(see p85)*, this family-friendly resort's prime location is complemented by a glorious outdoor pool surrounded by verdant gardens. The dining experience includes the Mediterranean-themed Il Basílico Restaurant.

Pousada Palácio de Estói

MAP K5 ■ Palácio de Estói, Estói ■ (289) 990 150 ■ www.pousadas.pt ■ €€
The ancestral home of the Viscount of Estói has been carefully renovated. A contemporary wing was attached to create a luxurious pousada with ceiling murals, a spa, a swimming pool and French gardens.

Tivoli Carvoeiro

MAP E5 ■ Vale do Covo, Carvoeiro ■ (282) 351 100 ■ www.tivolihotels.com ■ €€
Commanding views over precipitous cliffs, this hotel is within walking distance of Carvoeiro town centre. The interior is Moorish in influence, and some rooms have spectacular ocean vistas. The health club has a Jacuzzi, sauna and Turkish bath, and there is a diving school nearby.

Tivoli Lagos

MAP D5 ■ Rua António Crisógono dos Santos, Lagos ■ (282) 790 079 ■ www.tivolihotels.com ■ €€
Near the old town, this smart hotel comprises a series of buildings set around a swimming pool. Guests also have the use of an exclusive beach club on the seafront.

Vila Monte

MAP L5 ■ Sítio dos Caliços, Moncarapacho ■ (289) 790 790 ■ www.vilamonte.com ■ €€
A rustic-chic design defines this upmarket boutique property, located 15 minutes inland from the beach. Housed in different buildings, the rooms and suites are stylishly furnished. Guest amenities extend to the homely À Terra restaurant *(see p95)*. Other activities include yoga, hiking, horseback riding, golf lessons and dolphin-watching.

Value for Money

Albergaria Vila Lido

MAP E5 ■ Avenida Tomás Cabreira, Praia da Rocha ■ (282) 424 127 ■ Closed mid-Oct–Mar ■ www.vilalido.pt ■ €
Overlooking the beach, this charming villa, with its distinctive blue window shutters, exudes grace and elegance. Rooms are light and airy and offer either sea or garden views. Breakfast is eaten on a beautiful veranda.

Alte Hotel

MAP H3 ■ Estrada de Santa Margarida, Alte ■ (289) 478 523 ■ www.hotelinalgarve.top ■ €
Alte is one of the prettiest villages in the Algarve, surrounded by the Serra do Caldeirão mountains. The views from the hotel are stunning, although its position at the summit of a hill means that having your own transport is useful. Leisure amenities include a swimming pool, tennis court and billiards.

Hotel Colina dos Mouros

MAP F4 ■ Pocinho Santo, Silves ■ (282) 340 470 ■ Closed Nov–Mar ■ www.colinahotels.com ■ €
There is a great view of Silves castle from this friendly hotel, just a few minutes' walk from the historic quarter. A sun terrace overlooks a circular pool and rows of orange groves.

Hotel Residencial Salema

MAP C5 ■ Rua 28 de Janeiro, Salema ■ (282) 695 328 ■ www.hotelsalema.com ■ €
The hotel building is the centrepiece of an old quay that retains the charm of colourful boats and rows of fishermen's huts. The rooms have views of the bay, and there are many bars, restaurants and cafés nearby.

Loulé Jardim

MAP J4 ■ Praça Manuel de Arriaga, 8100 Loulé ■ (289) 413 094 ■ www.loulejardimhotel.com ■ €
Refurbished to an early 20th-century design, the mustard-and-cream façade faces a quiet park in the centre of Loulé. The town's castle and Saturday market are both within easy reach, and the rooftop pool is a bonus.

Alcazar Hotel

MAP P4 ■ Rua de Ceuta 9, Monte Gordo ■ (281) 510 140 ■ www.hotelalcazaralgarve.com ■ €€
With clean and comfortable beachfront rooms, this

hotel is ideal for couples. It has won praise for its excellent customer service and hearty breakfasts. There is a bar and two outdoor pools. A perfect base from which to explore the eastern Algarve.

Casa da Moura

MAP D5 ■ Rua Cardeal Neto 10, Lagos ■ (967) 177 590 ■ www.casadamoura.com ■ €€

The interior design of this 100-year-old manor house reflects a colourful Moorish style. A tiled patio garden surrounds a small swimming pool. The breakfast terrace affords fine views over the old town walls.

Vila São Vicente

MAP G5 ■ Largo Jacinto D'Ayet, Albufeira ■ (289) 583 700 ■ www.hotelsaovicentealbufeira.com ■ €€

This traditionally-styled boutique property has rooms with terraces or balconies, and some with glorious ocean views. A modest swimming pool is sunk into the outside patio. The beach, old town and marina *(see p37)* are a 10-minute walk away.

Budget Hotels

Casa Beny

MAP J4 ■ Rua São Domingos 13, Loulé ■ (289) 417 702 ■ No credit cards ■ Breakfast not included ■ €

A smart property, located in the centre of Loulé. The sleek, well-appointed rooms all have a TV and fridge, and guests also have access to a very handy rooftop terrace, where superb views of the castle can be enjoyed.

Pensão Bicuar Residencial

MAP L5 ■ Rua Vasco da Gama 5, Olhão ■ (289) 714 816 ■ No credit cards ■ No air conditioning ■ www.pensionbicuar.com ■ €

Centrally located, this self-catering budget option offers different room categories, all with a private shower. There is a fully equipped guest kitchen and Wi-Fi.

Pensão Luar

MAP C1 ■ Rua da Várzea 28, Odeceixe ■ (282) 947 194 ■ No credit cards ■ No air conditioning ■ €

Some of the rooms here overlook the sweeping River Seixe valley, and this friendly *pensão* is ideal for the beach at Odeceixe. While secluded, this area is popular in summer, so booking is advisable.

Residência Matos Pereira

MAP P4 ■ Rua Dr Sousa Martins 57, Vila Real de Santo António ■ (281) 543 325 ■ No credit cards ■ Air conditioning in some rooms ■ www.residenciamatospereira.com ■ €

Set in a pedestrianized street, the Residência looks like a typical town house, and is matched by an atmosphere that is both domestic and jovial.

Residencial Lagôas

MAP M4 ■ Rua Almirante Cândido dos Reis 24, Tavira ■ (281) 328 243 ■ No credit cards ■ No air conditioning ■ €

Polished black and white *azulejos* adorn the façade of this *pensão*. Its proximity to the historic centre of Tavira makes it very popular in summer, so telephone ahead to check room availability.

Residencial Miradouro da Serra

MAP E3 ■ Rua Combatentes do Ultramar, Monchique ■ (969) 158 301 ■ No air conditioning ■ www.miradourodaserra.com ■ €

The hotel name means "mountain viewpoint" and the panorama from this hilltop hideaway does not disappoint. The rooms are excellent value and the place makes a great base for hill walking or for simply pottering about in the pleasant market town of Monchique. All rooms have balcony views.

Residencial Pensão Limas

MAP G5 ■ Rua da Liberdade, 25–7, Albufeira ■ (289) 514 025 ■ No credit cards ■ Breakfast not included ■ €

Wedged between bars and restaurants in a narrow, pedestrianized street, Limas's bright yellow awnings grace a whitewashed façade. The staircase inside is steep and narrow, and leads to modest bedrooms.

Residencial Ponte Romana

MAP F4 ■ Ponte Romana, Silves ■ (282) 443 275 ■ No credit cards ■ Breakfast not included ■ €

Standing by the Roman bridge on the south side of the River Arade, this location is hard to beat. The riverside rooms face the castle. The restaurant serves generous portions of delicious country food.

***For a key to hotel price categories** see p124*

Sol Algarve

MAP K6 ■ Rua Infante D. Henrique 52, Faro ■ (289) 895 700 ■ www.hotelsolalgarve.com ■ €

All 38 rooms at this cheery establishment are en suite, and most have a balcony. When it is sunny, breakfast can be eaten in an attractive inner courtyard.

Casa Azul

MAP B6 ■ Rua D. Sebastião, Sagres ■ (282) 624 856 ■ €€

Stylish, bright and colourful, this superior guesthouse has captured the imagination of surfers and city slickers alike. Its central position makes it ideal for Sagres' buzzing nightlife. Advance booking is recommended.

Character Hostels and B&Bs

Amazigh Design Hostel

MAP C3 ■ Rua da Ladeira 5, Aljezur ■ (282) 997 502 ■ Breakfast not included ■ www.amazighostel.com ■ €

A stylish budget option configured with multi-bed dorms and private double rooms, all heated and with private bathrooms. A fully equipped kitchen provides self-catering facilities. Common areas have free Wi-Fi and plasma TVs.

City Stork Hostel

MAP E4 ■ Rua Direita 70, Portimão ■ (962) 327 792 ■ www.citystorkhostel.com ■ €

Family-run and named after the white storks nesting on a nearby chimneystack, the hostel enjoys a great location near the riverfront. The double rooms and dorms have their own bathroom facilities, but guests share a kitchen. Breakfast is included in the price.

Loulé Coreto Hostel

MAP J4 ■ Avenida José da Costa Mealha 68, Loulé ■ (966) 660 943 ■ www.loulecoretohostel.com ■ €

Male and female dorms and private rooms are available in a quiet and tastefully decorated environment, serviced to hotel standards. Bathroom and kitchen facilities are shared, and a buffet breakfast is served daily.

Quinta da Tapada do Gramacho

MAP E4 ■ Sítio Tapada do Gramacho, Silves ■ (919) 667 048 ■ Closed Nov–Mar ■ www.tapadadogramacho.com ■ €

A traditional farmhouse has been renovated into this chic, rustic hideaway. Comprising of uniquely designed, en suite, self-catering apartments and B&B suites, the *quinta*'s amenities extend to a communal kitchen and lounge, and an exterior swimming pool.

Casa Beleza do Sul

MAP M4 ■ Rua Doutor Parreira 43, Tavira ■ (960) 060 906 ■ www.casabelezadosul.com ■ €€

Three suites and one studio, all with a kitchenette, occupy this lovingly restored, 19th-century town house. Individually styled and utterly beguiling, each room has access to a patio terrace. There is also a larger roof terrace with wonderful views. Breakfast is optional.

Casa Modesta

MAP L5 ■ Quatrim do Sul, near Olhão ■ (289) 701 096/(964) 738 824 ■ www.casamodesta.pt ■ €€

A striking example of a modern makeover, this lovely guesthouse set in countryside over-looking the Ria Formosa Estuary has nine suites, some with a private ter-race and a kitchenette. The garden features a pool and a solarium. Dinner is prepared on request.

Casa Rosada

MAP P3 ■ Rua Dr Silvestre Falcão 6-10, Castro Marim ■ (281) 544 215 ■ No credit cards ■ www.casarosada-algarve.com ■ €€

A tangible air of tranquillity pervades Casa Rosada's interior, and with just three individually furnished bed-rooms provided, its appeal is delightfully understated. It is ideal for couples, who are welcomed as family. Breakfast is healthy and wholesome and served in the garden.

Quinta do Mel

MAP G5 ■ Olhos D'Água, Albufeira ■ (289) 543 674 ■ www.quintadomel.com ■ €€

This secluded rural retreat offers ten attrac-tive rooms, each with a private bathroom. Comforts include TV and free internet. A pool is set in the landscaped grounds, artisan farm produce is sold in the teashop and a restau-rant complements the breakfast offer.

Vilafoîa

MAP E3 ■ Corte Pereiro, Monchique ■ (282) 910 110 ■ www.vilafoia.com ■ €€

A smart, modern B&B option set deep in woodland and ideal for exploring the Monchique hills. Rooms and studios are well appointed and enjoy splendid countryside views. The well-manicured gardens feature a salt-water swimming pool.

Campsites

Albufeira Camping

MAP G5 ■ Estrada de Ferreiras, Albufeira ■ (289) 587 629 ■ www.campingalbufeira.pt ■ €

A sprawling camping and caravan site about 2 km (1 mile) from town, with three pools, an adventure playground, an à la carte restaurant, a supermarket and a nightclub.

Camping Olhão

MAP L5 ■ Pinheiros de Marim, Apartado 300, Olhão ■ (289) 700 300 ■ €

This excellent site near the Parque Natural da Ria Formosa has first-class amenities and lively recreation facilities that include a swimming pool and a tennis court. There is also a mini-market, a restaurant and a bar.

Parque de Campismo de Armação de Pêra

MAP F5 ■ Parque de Campismo de Armação de Pêra ■ (282) 312 260 ■ www.camping-armacao-pera.com ■ €

The nearest campsite to Armação de Pêra, this is great for budget travellers who crave the sights and nightlife of a lively resort. Modern facilities abound and it is also possible to rent bungalows.

Parque de Campismo de Monte Gordo

MAP P4 ■ Monte Gordo ■ (281) 510 970 ■ www.cm-vrsa.pt ■ €

The conifer woodland near this campsite is home to the largest population of Mediterranean chameleon in Portugal. The walks here are superb, and Monte Gordo itself is a thriving town with a beach that has perfect conditions for sunbathing and swimming.

Parque de Campismo Muncipal da Ilha de Tavira

MAP M5 ■ Ilha de Tavira ■ (281) 320 580 ■ Closed Oct–May ■ No credit cards ■ €

This island is car- and caravan-free; only tents are allowed. There are supermarket and restaurant facilities, and tent hire is possible too. The island is reached via ferry at Quatro Águas. The site is hugely popular in summer, so it is definitely best to book ahead.

Parque de Campismo Sagres

MAP B6 ■ Cerro das Moitas, Sagres ■ (282) 624 371 ■ www.orbitur.pt ■ €

It is not uncommon to see surfboards outside the tents and cabins here, as the campsite is within easy reach of some very fine surfing beaches. The amenities are excellent, and Sagres town is just less than 2 km (1 mile) away.

Parque de Campismo São Miguel

MAP C1 ■ São Miguel, near Odeceixe ■ (282) 947 145 ■ www.campingsaomiguel.com ■ €

Secluded under a canopy of pine, this is one of the most modern and well-equipped camping sites in southern Portugal. Facilities include tennis courts, a swimming pool, a supermarket and a restaurant, and the surrounding countryside is a national park. Sleek and modern caravans and bungalows can also be rented.

Parque de Campismo Serrão

MAP C3 ■ Herdade do Serrão, Aljezur ■ (282) 990 220 ■ www.campingserrao.com ■ €

This friendly camp and caravan site is conveniently located near some of the western Algarve's very best beaches. The facilities include a large swimming pool and a series of bungalows to rent, two of which offer wheelchair access.

Salema Eco Camp

MAP C5 ■ Parque de Campismo, Quinta dos Carriços, Praia da Salema, Budens ■ (282) 695 201 ■ www.salemaecocamp.com ■ €

Set in a pretty valley, this campsite offers all the necessary facilities – toilets, hot showers, laundry rooms, shops and a restaurant. There are modern studios and apartments for rent as well as the tent pitches.

***For a key to hotel price categories** see p124*

General Index

Page numbers in **bold** refer to main entries

Acknowledgments

Author

Paul Bernhardt is a freelance travel writer, blogger and photographer who lives in Portugal.

Publishing Director Georgina Dee

Publisher Vivien Antwi

Design Director Phil Ormerod

Editorial Sophie Adam, Michelle Crane, Dipika Dasgupta, Rebecca Flynn, Rachel Fox, Ruth Reisenberger, Sally Schafer

Cover Design Bess Daly, Maxine Pedliham

Design Rahul Kumar, Marisa Renzullo

Picture Research Susie Peachey, Ellen Root, Lucy Sienkowska, Oran Tarjan

Cartography Zafar-ul-Islam Khan, Suresh Kumar, James Macdonald, Casper Morris

DTP Jason Little

Production Nancy-Jane Maun

Factchecker Mark Harding

Proofreader Laura Walker

Indexer Hilary Bird

First edition created by Blue Island Publishing, London

Revisions Marc Di Duca, Ben Hinks, Sumita Khatwani, Bharti Karakoti, Shikha Kulkarni, Bandana Paul, Vagisha Pushp, Kanika Praharaj, Anuroop Sanwalia, Ankita Sharma, Priyanka Thakur, Beverly Smart, Vinita Venugopal, Danielle Watt, Tanveer Zaidi

Commissioned Photography Paul Bernhardt, Will Heap, William Reavell, Rough Guides/ Eddie Gerald, Matthew Hancock, Linda Whitwam

Picture Credits

The publisher would like to thank the following for their kind permission to reproduce their photographs:

Key: a-above; b-below/bottom; c-centre; f-far; l-left; r-right; t-top

123RF.com: lianem 110b.

4Corners: Michael Howard 45b, 60b; SIME/ Olimpio Fantuz 49cr, 56t.

À Terra, Vila Monte: Nick Bayntun 95cra.

Adega do Cantor: Birchphotography.com/Dan Birch 37tl, 54br.

Alamy Stock Photo: age fotostock/Salva Garrigues 31tr; Arco Images GmbH 44bc, / Therin-Weise 18-9; The Art Archive/Gianni Dagli Orti 42br; Greg Balfour Evans 7tl, 74b, 88b; Paul Bernhardt 14crb; Bildagentur-online 16-7; blickwinkel/McPHOTO/ZAG 48tr; Ian Bottle 50cra; Buiten-Beeld/Nico van Kappel 33tr; Andy Christiani 10cb; Carl DeAbreu 27cra; DIGITEYES 2tr, 40-1; edpics 10tr; eye35 34-5, 104tl; eye35 stock 45cla; eye35.pix 3tr, 27tl, 114-5; Stephen French 10b; Gastromedia/Gastrofotos 68bl; GM Photo Images 16bl; hemis.fr/Philippe Blanchot 54tr; The History Collection 43tl; Jam World Images 4cla; Christa Knijff 42cla; Hideo Kurihara 111br; Kuttig - RF - Travel 2tl, 8-9; LH Images 64crb; LOOK Die Bildagentur der Fotografen GmbH 22clb; LusoWine 112t; Johnny Madsen 32br; Cro Magnon 4clb, 4b, 17crb, 38clb, 46br, 47tl, 92b, 108bl; mauritius images GmbH 67b; Stephen Meese 11cb; MicaSelects 38-9; Mikehoward 2 67tr; tony mills 32tl; Novarc Images/Miguel Caibarien 43br; pbucknall 58b; LOOK Die Bildagentur der Fotografen GmbH/ Roetting/ Pollex 19tl; Simon Reddy 69clb; Phil Rees 74cl; Robertharding/Neale Clark 35tc; Mauro Rodrigues 76tl; Rymar 23br; Kumar Sriskandan 18cl; Travel Pictures/Pictures Colour Library 50bl; travelpixs 28t; 39clb; Duncan Usher 32c; Visions from Earth 62-3, 96–7; Washington Imaging 4t; Westend61 GmbH/Mel Stuart 31bl, /Michael Reusse 57cla; Jan Wlodarczyk 4crb.

Algarve Classic Car Festival: 77br.

Apolónia Supermercados: 87br.

Associação Turismo do Algarve: 20-1, 57bl, 94b, 98tl.

Autodromo Internacional de Algarve: A. Fernandes 38br.

AWL Images: Marco Bottigelli 1; Sabine Lubenow 60tl.

Paul Bernhardt: 13tl, 17tc.

Boutique Hotel Vivenda Miranda: 70br.

Cacto: 105cl.

Câmara Municipal de Lagos: Carlos Afonso 28bl, Lagos Museu Municipal 29cl.

Casa Velha: 70tl.

Corbis: Lou Avers 15c; JAI/Mauricio Abreu 100b; Wolfgang Kaehler 29tr.

Dreamstime.com: Ahfotobox 103b; Ilia Aleksandrov 85tr; Altezza 6cla, 12clb; Amabrao 61crb; Anitasstudio 48b; Anyaivanova 83cl; Philip Bird 91bl; Yuriy Brykaylo 66clb; Olena Buyskykh 102cl; Valeria Cantone 55crb; Roland Nagy 15bl; Carlos Neto 93cl; Dmitry Chulov 90tl; Wessel Cirkel 58cla; Compuinfoto 11tl, 75br; Cw24044 4t; Devy 26cra, 99t; Rene Drouyer 81t; Peter Etchells 26clb; Fabiomsantos 30-1, Ferragudo in the Algarve Portugal 51t; Fosterss 77cl; Armando Frazão 16cl; G0r3cki 30cl; Rafał Gadomski 10cla, 34clb; Golasza 4cl; Hectorsnchz 107b; Marianne De Jong 100tl; Joyfull 57tr; Jacek Kadaj 99cr; Lianem 109cl, 110cla; Madrugadaverde 3tl, 78-9; Mkos83 24-5; Aitor Muñoz Muñoz 35crb, 108t;

Murdock2013 20cra; Elena Pavlova 65br; Pkazmierczak 26br, 44cla, 51clb, 52-3; Ppy2010ha 68cla; Presse750 12br; Radaway 38cla; Mauro Rodrigues 4cr, 59clb; Ruigouveia 82-3; Saiko3p 12-3c, 106cla, 107tr; Rui G. Santos 54b; Sebastian423 84cl; Richard Semik 109bl; Sergioua 101cl; Ronalds Stikans 11bl; Stefano Valeri 71cla; Vvoevale 14tl; Steve Woods 22-3; Rudmer Zwerver 59br.

Getty Images: AWL Images RM/Sabine Lubenow 56bl; Paul Bernhardt 73crb; Valter Jacinto 33br; Keystone-France/Gamma-Keystone 43clb; Sabine Lubenow 11cra, 91tr; VWB photos 7cra.

Museu do Traje e São Brás de Alportel: 47br.

O Charneco: 89tr.

Photoshot: Frank Fell 21c.

Pine Cliffs: 86t.

Porches Pottery: Brian P. Fortune 75c, 87c.

Pousadas de Portugal/Grupo Pestana: 113cl.

Quinta do Francês vineyard: 72cl.

Rex by Shutterstock: imageBROKER/Jürgen Wackenhut 59tl.

Robert Harding Picture Library: BAO 15tr, 92tl; Neale Clark 11tr, 36cla; Jurgen Wackenhut 11crb; Jan Wlodarczyk 36-7.

Slide and Splash: 65t.

SuperStock: Stock Connection 85br.

Turismo de Portugal: Jose Manuel 12cla.

Vila Joya: 71crb.

Cover

Front and spine: **AWL Images:** Marco Bottigelli.

Back: **AWL Images:** Sabine Lubenow tr; **Dreamstime.com:** Artem Evdokimov cla; Hlphoto tl; Rosshelen crb; **AWL Images:** Marco Bottigelli b.

Pull Out Map Cover

AWL Images: Marco Bottigelli

All other images © Dorling Kindersley For further information see: www.dkimages.com

Printed and bound in China

First edition 2003
First published in Great Britain by
Dorling Kindersley Limited
DK, One Embassy Gardens, 8 Viaduct
Gardens, London SW11 7BW, UK

Published in the United States by
DK US, 1450 Broadway, Suite 801
New York, NY 10018, USA

A Penguin Random House Company
21 22 23 24 10 9 8 7 6 5 4 3 2 1

Reprinted with revisions 2005, 2007, 2009, 2011, 2013, 2015, 2017, 2019, 2021

A CIP catalogue record is available from the British Library.

A catalogue record for this book is available from the Library of Congress.

ISSN 1479-344X
ISBN 978-0-2414-6295-9

As a guide to abbreviations in visitor information blocks: ***Adm*** *= admission charge;* ***D*** *= dinner;* ***L*** *= lunch.*

Phrase Book

In an Emergency

Help!	Socorro!	soo-koh-roo!
Stop!	Pára!	pahr'!
Call a doctor!	Chame um médico!	shahm' ooñ meh-dee-koo!
Call an ambulance!	Chame uma ambulância!	shahm' oo-muh añ-boo-lañ-see-uh!
Call the police!	Chame a polícia!	shahm' uh poo-lee-see-uh!
Call the fire brigade!	Chame os bombeiros!	shahm' oosh' bom-bay-roosh!
Where is the nearest telephone?	Há um telefone aqui perto?	ah ooñ te-le-fon' uh-kee pehr-too?
Where is the nearest hospital?	Onde é o hospital mais próximo?	ond' eh oo ohsh-pee-tahl' mysh pro-see-moo?

Communication Essentials

Yes	Sim	seeñ
No	Não	nowñ
Please	Por favor/ Faz favor	poor fuh-vor fash fuh-vor
Thank you	Obrigado/da	o-bree-gah-doo/duh
Excuse me	Desculpe	dish-koolp'
Hello	Olá	oh-lah
Goodbye	Adeus	a-deh-oosh
Good morning	Bom-dia	boñ dee-uh
Good afternoon	Boa-tarde	boh-uh tard'
Good night	Boa-noite	boh-uh noyt'
Yesterday	Ontem	oñ-tayñ
Today	Hoje	ohj'
Tomorrow	Amanhã	ah-mañ yañ
Here	Aqui	uh-kee
There	Ali	uh-lee
What?	O quê?	oo keh?
Which?	Qual?	kwahl'?
When?	Quando?	kwañ-doo?
Why?	Porquê?	poor-keh?
Where?	Onde?	oñd'?

Useful Phrases

How are you?	Como está?	koh-moo shtah?
Very well, thank you.	Bem, obrigado/da.	bayñ, o-bree gah-doo/duh.
Pleased to meet you.	Encantado/da.	eñ-kañ-tah-doo/ duh.
See you soon.	Até logo.	uh-teh loh-goo.
That's fine.	Está bem.	shtah bayñ.
Where is/are…?	Onde está/ estão…?	ond' shtah/ shtowñ...?
How far is it to…?	A que distância fica…?	uh kee dish-tañ-see-uh fee-kuh...?
Which way to…?	Como se vai para…?	koh-moo seh vy puh-ruh...?
Do you speak English?	Fala Inglês?	fah-luh eeñ-glehsh?
I don't understand.	Não compreendo.	nowñ kom-pree-eñ-doo.
I'm sorry.	Desculpe.	dish-koolp'
Could you speak more slowly, please?	Pode falar mais devagar, por favor?	pohd' fuh-lar mysh d'-va-gar, poor fah-vor?

Useful Words

big	grande	grañd'
small	pequeno	pe-keh-noo
hot	quente	keñt'
cold	frio	free-oo
good	bom	boñ
bad	mau	mah-oo
enough	bastante	bash-tañt'
well	bem	bayñ
open	aberto	a-behr-too
closed	fechado	fe-shah-doo
left	esquerda	shkehr-duh
right	direita	dee-ray-tuh
straight on	em frente	ayñ freñt'
near	perto	pehr-too
far	longe	loñj'
up	suba	soo-bah
down	desça	deh-shuh
early	cedo	seh-doo
late	tarde	tard'
entrance	entrada	eñ-trah-duh
exit	saída	sa-ee-duh
toilets	casa de banho	kah-zuh d' bañ-yoo
more	mais	mysh
less	menos	meh-noosh

Making a Telephone Call

I'd like to place an international call.	Queria fazer uma chamada internacional.	kree-uh fuh-zehr oo-muh sha-mah-duh in-ter-na-see-oo-nahl'.
a local call	uma chamada local	oo-muh sha-mah-duh loo-kahl'
Can I leave a message?	Posso deixar uma mensagem?	poh-soo day-shar oo-muh meñ-sah-jayñ?

Shopping

How much does this cost?	Quanto custa isto?	kwañ-too koosh-tuh eesh-too?
I would like…	Queria…	kree-uh...
I'm just looking.	Estou só a ver obrigado/a.	shtoh soh uh vehr o-bree-gah-doo/uh.
Do you take credit cards?	Aceita cartões de crédito?	uh-say-tuh kar-toinsh de kreh-dee-too?
What time do you open?	A que horas abre?	uh kee oh-rash ah-bre?
What time do you close?	A que horas fecha?	uh kee oh-rash fay-shuh?
this one	este	ehst'
that one	esse	ehss'
expensive	caro	kah-roo
cheap	barato	buh-rah-too
size (clothes/ shoes)	número	noom'-roo
white	branco	brañ-koo
black	preto	preh-too
red	vermelho	ver-melh-yoo
yellow	amarelo	uh-muh-reh-loo
green	verde	vehrd'
blue	azul	uh-zool'

Types of Shop

antique shop	**loja de antiguidades**	*__loh__-juh de añ-tee-gwee-dahd'sh*
bakery	**padaria**	*pah-duh-__ree__-uh*
bank	**banco**	*__bañ__-koo*
bookshop	**livraria**	*lee-vruh-__ree__-uh*
butcher	**talho**	*__tah__-lyoo*
cake shop	**pastelaria**	*pash-te-luh-__ree__-uh*
chemist	**farmácia**	*far-__mah__-see-uh*
fishmonger	**peixaria**	*pay-shuh-__ree__-uh*
hairdresser	**cabeleireiro**	*kab'-lay-__ray__-roo*
market	**mercado**	*mehr-__kah__-doo*
newsagent	**kiosque**	*kee-__yohsk'__*
post office	**correios**	*koo-__ray__-oosh*
shoe shop	**sapataria**	*suh-puh-tuh-__ree__-uh*
supermarket	**supermercado**	*soo-__pehr__-mer-__kah__-doo*
tobacconist	**tabacaria**	*tuh-buh-kuh-__ree__-uh*
travel agency	**agência de viagens**	*uh-jen-__see__-uh de vee-__ah__-jayñsh*

Sightseeing

cathedral	**sé**	*__seh__*
church	**igreja**	*ee-__gray__-juh*
garden	**jardim**	*jar-__deeñ__*
library	**biblioteca**	*bee-blee-oo-__teh__-kuh*
museum	**museu**	*__moo__-zeh-oo*
tourist information	**posto de turismo**	*posh-__too__ d' too-__reesh__-moo*
closed for holidays	**fechado para férias**	*fe-__sha__-doo puh-ruh __feh__-ree-ash*
bus station	**estação de autocarros**	*shta-sowñ d' oh-too-__kah__-roosh*
railway station	**estação de comboios**	*shta-__sowñ__ d' koñ-__boy__-oosh*
painted ceramic tile	**azulejo**	*uh-zoo-lay-joo*
Manueline (late Gothic architectural style)	**Manuelino**	*ma-noo-el-ee-oo*

Staying in a Hotel

Do you have a vacant room?	**Tem um quarto livre?**	*__tayñ__ ooñ __kwar__-too __leevr'__?*
room with a bath	**um quarto com casa de banho**	*ooñ __kwar__-too koñ __kah__-zuh d' bañ-__yoo__*
shower	**duche**	*__doosh__*
single room	**quarto individual**	*__kwar__-too een-dee-vee-doo-__ahl'__*
double room	**quarto de casal**	*__kwar__-too d' kuh-__zhal'__*
twin room	**quarto com duas camas**	*__kwar__-too koñ __doo__-ash __kah__-mash*
porter	**porteiro**	*poor-__tay__-roo*
key	**chave**	*__shahv'__*
I have a reservation.	**Tenho um quarto reservado.**	*__tayñ__-yoo ooñ __kwar__-too re-ser-__vah__-doo.*

Eating Out

Have you got a table for …?	**Tem uma mesa para … ?**	*__tayñ__ oo-muh __meh__-zuh puh-ruh?*
I'd like to reserve a table.	**Quero reservar una mesa.**	*__keh__-roo re-zehr-__var__ oo-muh __meh__-zuh.*
The bill, please.	**A conta por favor/faz favor.**	*uh __kohn__-tuh poor fuh-__vor__/ __fash__ fuh-__vor.__*
I am a vegetarian.	**Sou vegetariano/a.**	*Soh ve-je-tuh-ree-__ah__-noo/uh.*
Waiter!	**Por favor!/ Faz favor!**	*poor fuh-__vor__! __fash__ fuh-__vor__!*
the menu	**a lista**	*uh __leesh__-tuh*
fixed-price menu	**a ementa turística**	*uh ee-__mehñ__-tuh too-__reesh__-tee-kuh*
wine list	**a lista de vinhos**	*uh __leesh__-tuh de __veeñ__-yoosh*
glass	**um copo**	*ooñ __koh__-poo*
bottle	**uma garrafa**	*oo-muh guh-__rah__-fuh*
half-bottle	**meia-garrafa**	*__may__-uh guh-__rah__-fuh*
knife	**uma faca**	*oo-mah __fah__-kuh*
fork	**um garfo**	*ooñ __gar__-foo*
spoon	**uma colher**	*oo-muh kool-__yair__*
plate	**um prato**	*ooñ __prah__-too*
breakfast	**pequeno-almoço**	*pe-__keh__-noo-ahl-__moh__-soo*
lunch	**almoço**	*ahl-__moh__-soo*
dinner	**jantar**	*jan-__tar__*
cover	**couvert**	*koo-__vehr__*
starter	**entrada**	*eñ-__trah__-duh*
main course	**prato principal**	*__prah__-too prin-see-__pahl'__*
dish of the day	**prato do dia**	*__prah__-too doo __dee__-uh*
set dish	**combinado**	*koñ-bee-__nah__-doo*
half-portion	**meia-dose**	*may-uh __doh__-se*
dessert	**sobremesa**	*__soh__-bre-__meh__-zuh*
rare	**mal passado**	*__mahl'__ puh-__sah__- doo*
medium	**médio**	*__meh__-dee-oo*
well done	**bem passado**	*__bayñ__ puh-__sah__- doo*

Menu Decoder

abacate	*uh-buh-__kaht'__*	avocado
açorda	*uh-__sor__-duh*	bread-based stew (often seafood)
açúcar	*uh-soo-__kar__*	sugar
água mineral	*__ah__-gwuh mee-ne-__rahl'__*	mineral water
alho	*__ay__-oo*	garlic
alperce	*ahl'-__pehrce__*	apricot
amêijoas	*uh-may-__joo__-ash*	clams
ananás	*uh-nuh-__nahsh__*	pineapple
arroz	*uh-__rohsh__*	rice
assado	*uh-__sah__-doo*	baked
atum	*uh-__tooñ__*	tuna
aves	*__ah__-vesh*	poultry
azeite	*uh-__zayt'__*	olive oil
azeitonas	*uh-zay-__toh__-nash*	olives
bacalhau	*buh-kuh-__lyow__*	dried, salted cod
banana	*buh-__nah__-nuh*	banana
batatas	*buh-__tah__-tash*	potatoes
batatas fritas	*buh-__tah__-tash __free__-tash*	French fries

batido	*buh-**tee**-doo*	milkshake
bica	***bee**-kuh*	espresso
bife	***beef***	steak
bolacha	*boo-**lah**-shuh*	biscuit
bolo	***boh**-loo*	cake
borrego	*boo-**reh**-goo*	lamb
caça	***kah**-ssuh*	game
café	*kuh-**feh***	coffee
camarões	*kuh-muh-**roysh***	large prawns
caracóis	*kuh-ruh-**koysh***	snails
caranguejo	*kuh-rañ **gay**-yoo*	crabs
carne	***karn'***	meat
cataplana	*kuh-tuh-**plah**-nah*	sealed wok used to steam dishes
cebola	*se-**boh**-luh*	onion
cerveja	*sehr-**vay**-juh*	beer
chá	***shah***	tea
cherne	***shern'***	stone bass
chocolate	*shoh-koh-**laht'***	chocolate
chocos	***shoh**-koosh*	cuttlefish
chouriço	*shoh-**ree**-soo*	red, spicy sausage
churrasco	*shoo-**rash**-coo*	on the spit
cogumelos	*koo-goo-**meh**-loosh*	mushrooms
cozido	*koo-**zee**-doo*	boiled
enguias	*eñ-**gee**-ash*	eels
fiambre	*fee-**añbr'***	ham
figado	***fee**-guh-doo*	liver
frango	***frañ**-goo*	chicken
frito	***free**-too*	fried
fruta	***froo**-tuh*	fruit
gambas	***gañ**-bash*	prawns
gelado	*je-**lah**-doo*	ice cream
gelo	*jeh-**loo***	ice
goraz	*goo-**rash***	bream
grelhado	*grel-**yah**-doo*	grilled
iscas	***eesh**-kash*	marinated liver
lagosta	*luh-**gohsh**-tuh*	lobster
laranja	*luh **rañ**-juh*	orange
leite	***layt'***	milk
limão	*lee-**mowñ***	lemon
limonada	*lee-moo-**nah**-duh*	lemonade
linguado	*leeñ-**gwah**-doo*	sole
lulas	***loo**-lash*	squid
maçã	*muh-**sañ***	apple
manteiga	*mañ-**tay**-guh*	butter
marisco	*muh-**reesh**-koosh*	seafood
meia-de-leite	***may**-uh-d' **layt'***	white coffee
ostras	***osh**-trash*	oysters
ovos	***oh**-voosh*	eggs
pão	***powñ***	bread
pastel	*pash-**tehl'***	cake
pato	***pah**-too*	duck
peixe	***paysh'***	fish
peixe-espada	***paysh'**-**shpah**-duh*	scabbard fish
pimenta	*pee-**meñ**-tuh*	pepper
polvo	***pohl'**-voo*	octopus
porco	***por**-coo*	pork
queijo	***kay**-joo*	cheese
sal	***sahl'***	salt
salada	*suh-**lah**-duh*	salad
salsichas	*sahl-**see**-shash*	sausages
sandes	***sañ**-desh*	sandwich
sopa	***soh**-puh*	soup
sumo	***soo**-moo*	juice
tamboril	*tañ-boo-**ril'***	monkfish
tarte	***tart'***	pie/cake
tomate	*too-**maht'***	tomato
torrada	*too-**rah**-duh*	toast
tosta	***tohsh**-tuh*	toasted sandwich
vinagre	*vee-**nah**-gre*	vinegar
vinho branco	***veeñ**-yoo **brañ**-koo*	white wine
vinho tinto	***veeñ**-yoo **teeñ**-too*	red wine
vitela	*vee-**teh**-luh*	veal

Numbers

0	zero	***zeh**-roo*
1	um	***ooñ***
2	dois	***doysh***
3	três	***tresh***
4	quatro	***kwa**-troo*
5	cinco	***seeñ**-koo*
6	seis	***saysh***
7	sete	***set'***
8	oito	***oy**-too*
9	nove	***nov'***
10	dez	***desh***
11	onze	***oñz'***
12	doze	***doz'***
13	treze	***trez'***
14	catorze	*ka-**torz'***
15	quinze	***keeñz'***
16	dezasseis	*de-zuh-**saysh***
17	dezassete	*de-zuh-**set'***
18	dezoito	*de-**zoy**-too*
19	dezanove	*de-zuh-**nov'***
20	vinte	***veent'***
21	vinte e um	***veen-tee**-ooñ*
30	trinta	***treeñ**-tuh*
40	quarenta	*kwa-**reñ**-tuh*
50	cinquenta	*seen-**kweñ**-tuh*
60	sessenta	*se-**señ**-tuh*
70	setenta	*se-**teñ**-tuh*
80	oitenta	*oy-**teñ**-tuh*
90	noventa	*noo-**veñ**-tuh*
100	cem	***sayñ***
101	cento e um	***señ**-too-ee-ooñ*
102	cento e dois	***señ**-too-ee-**doysh***
200	duzentos	*doo-**zeñ**-toosh*
300	trezentos	*tre-**zeñ**-toosh*
400	quatrocentos	***kwa**-troo-**señ**-toosh*
500	quinhentos	*kee-**nyeñ**-toosh*
600	seiscentos	*saysh-**señ**-toosh*
700	setecentos	*set'-**señ**-toosh*
800	oitocentos	***oy**-too-**señ**-toosh*
900	novecentos	*nov'-**señ**-toosh*
1,000	mil	***meel'***

Time

one minute	um minuto	*ooñ mee-**noo**-too*
one hour	uma hora	***oo**-muh **oh**-ruh*
half an hour	meia-hora	***may**-uh **oh**-ruh*
Monday	segunda-feira	*se-**goon**-duh-**fay**-ruh*
Tuesday	terça-feira	*ter-sa-**fay**-ruh*
Wednesday	quarta-feira	***kwar**-ta-**fay**-ruh*
Thursday	quinta-feira	***keen**-ta-**fay**-ruh*
Friday	sexta-feira	***say**-shta-**fay**-ruh*
Saturday	sábado	***sah**-ba-too*
Sunday	domingo	*doo-**meen**-goo*